The Interview

Roger Spielmann

13-Digit ISBN: 978-1-7770688-1-3

Dedication

To

My three beautiful daughters:
Jennifer, Melissa, and Stephanie.
You make my life worth living.

Chapter One

I*n the beginning,* why I was chosen to interview Jesus Christ was beyond me. I mean, really, I didn't know if I even *believed* in the guy. Like, I had a vague notion that there was a God of some sort, but then, who didn't? I wasn't brought up in a religious home, so I was never forced to go to church and never heard anything about God from my parents.

I believed in Santa Claus, though, so it's not like it would have been a huge leap of faith to believe in some invisible God who lived in the sky and kept a list of whether you were good or not.

But even that ended when I finally found out that *Santa Claus wasn't real.* My older sister let me in on the secret when I turned eight. So, yeah, it turned out Santa Claus was a big hoax foisted on kids to make them believe in a big, fat guy with a long white beard, wearing a red suit, who would bring toys and what have you to all the good little kids in the world (but not the bad ones), all the while riding in a big sled pulled by magical flying reindeer.

Right after learning that Santa was just a *big lie,* now I was supposed to believe in an invisible God who lived in the sky and amused himself by doing nice things for you if you were a good boy or girl and punishing you if you were bad? Fool me once, okay, but fool me twice with the same setup?

I don't think so.

* * *

For the next few years, the whole *God in the sky* story sounded loopy to me, so I didn't pay much attention to it. But then something really, really bad happened to me that caused me to think about God: my mom died in a car crash. I was twelve years old, and—*bang*—she was gone. *Omigod.* "How could God do that?" I wondered. Was it because of me?

I grew up on the South Side of Chicago. My dysfunctional family could have provided the story line for the TV show *Shameless*. After my mom died, my dad seemed to give up on life and started drinking heavily. I joined a gang and quickly began to get into a lot of trouble: stealing cars, vandalism, snatching purses, getting in fights, and drinking—that kind of thing. The gang I had joined was my new family, and I was pretty much a willing participant. By the time I was sixteen, our gang leader was in juvenile detention, and the rest of us were brought up on car-theft charges. As I waited for my court date, I remember feeling so down and alone that I looked out of my bedroom window and, for the first time in my life that I can remember, prayed. I said, "God, I don't know if you're really there, but if you are, please get me out of this mess."

I felt good that I had actually "talked" to God, whoever or whatever he was—was he even a he? Maybe a her? An it? However, more importantly, I soon found out that I was being given probation rather than sent to juvenile detention. I took that as a pretty sure sign that God, whoever he was, had heard my prayer, kind of like when my parents would take me to see the mall Santa, and amazingly, I actually got what I asked for at Christmas! (How did Santa do *that*?)

As I became older, I figured that maybe God would occasionally step in and get me out of trouble because he felt sorry for killing my mom. In my early twenties, I even did a short stint at a Bible college. I ended up dropping out after the first year. I learned a lot about the Bible, but my heart just wasn't in it. I had no interest in church either. I had seen and heard enough during my short stay at the Bible college to come to the point where I decided that religion just wasn't my thing. From that point on, I kind of figured my way through life, thinking about God every now and then but usually only when I was in trouble.

Mostly, though, I thought of my mom when I was in trouble. She somehow seemed to me more *real* than God, even though she was dead.

Chapter Two

By the time I hit my forties, I was near the end of my rope. I had spent the last twenty years or so bouncing around from job to job, just trying to earn enough money to support my ever-growing drug addiction. It's strange, though; my real reason for planning my own demise was because I was just so tired of living—sick and tired of being sick and tired all the time. My life was totally out of control; I was living most days in drug-induced withdrawal. I imagined what it would be like to end the sickness and pain and check out what happened after this life and, hopefully, to be reunited with my mom. I believed there was an afterlife of some sort where there was no more pain or suffering, no more feeling sick and tired all the time, always feeling good. I started to look forward to what I began thinking of as the greatest human adventure.

But first I had to get there.

My Internet research told me that carbon monoxide was the best way to go. Just drift away into oblivion. I brought my dog Poppy with me too. I couldn't stand the thought of her being without me. She'd been my faithful companion for fifteen years—through different girlfriends, places of abode, and vast and sundry experiences. I wanted us to go together. So I drove my car to a secluded spot and hooked a hose up to the exhaust pipe and through the rear window.

As I was drifting into unconsciousness, I could swear I heard a knocking on my car window—a hard, repeated knocking. I groggily opened my eyes, and sure enough, there were four police cars and an ambulance surrounding my car, along with two cops at my window. I managed to unlock the car door and was unceremoniously escorted to the ambulance. My "secluded" spot was evidently not as far off the beaten path as I thought. Somebody had seen my hooked-up car from the highway and called it in.

But where was Poppy? My last remembrance of her was when she was lying in the back seat, stretched out and sleeping peacefully. Was she still alive? If I had accidentally killed her, I would—well, I would kill myself. But there she was, prancing around the police officers' legs. She looked at me, scrunched down to pee, and yawned—just another day in the life of a dog.

My memories are vague and keep slipping away even now, but I do remember waking up in a single bed in the psych ward of the local hospital. The first few days I was in zombie mode, walking the halls aimlessly or sleeping. I also remember being very angry and confused. What the hell was happening? Why wasn't I dead? I was crushed.

I was put in a "lock down" room in the ward. The first few days I stayed in bed, and food was brought to me by nurses. I was so angry and confused. What the deal? Why wasn't I dead? After a few days, I began to stumble into the cafeteria at meal times and wandered the hallways at night. During the first week and a half, I refused to even see my assigned psychiatrist. After two weeks in, I was pretty much forced to see him if I ever wanted to get out of that place. Even so, I thought he was a complete prick. He just didn't "get it." In our first session, he asked me to make a list of the symptoms of opiate withdrawal. I told him no; the thing about withdrawal is that it's so horrible that you just want to be dead. I left that first meeting thinking the obvious, "Unless you've been in withdrawal, you'll never be able to understand it." Sounds like a cop-out, I know, but believe me, it's true.

I was given twenty minutes per day of computer access to check my e-mails. The first time on the computer, I had a string of e-mails from my three daughters, my elder sister, my brothers, and a few concerned friends. My partner Sylvie came to visit me every day, along with our close friend Heather. I learned to play the game with my shrink by telling him what I thought he wanted to hear so that I could get out of that hellhole. It eventually worked but only after some fancy word work and creative lying.

My three daughters, Daisy, Alison, and Jordyn, and well, everybody else too were stunned by my suicide attempt. My eldest, Daisy, had my back from the start. She understood my ongoing struggle with drugs and living much of the time in withdrawal. Jordyn, my youngest, basically followed Daisy's lead. They were just glad that "Dad" was still alive and kicking.

But my middle daughter, Alison, took it the hardest. She was upset beyond what I could even imagine. I was puzzled. Why didn't she feel the same way her sisters felt about the whole deal? I did put her through a lot of emotional turmoil prior to my suicide attempt, but her last e-mail to me while I was in the psych ward was devastating; she was not impressed with my decision to end it all and all the chaos that preceded it. She made it clear that she wanted no further contact with me.

I longed to be reconciled with Alison every day I was in the ward, hoping against hope for an e-mail telling me that I was forgiven. And every day my heartache increased.

It hurts to think about it even now. She told me she was washing her hands of me. She wanted no more contact until—well, she never really said. Indefinitely. I wondered if I would ever see her or talk to her again, ever. The very thought of being estranged from her made me want to kill myself all over again.

Chapter Three

I had been in the psych ward for two weeks before I met up with Joseph. He turned out to be one of the weirdest characters I'd ever met in my life. He really was a strange bird—a self-proclaimed chess master with no teeth, half-closed bloodshot eyes, and bedraggled hair. After a few days of seeing each other around the ward, we introduced ourselves and began spending time together at meals and break times, as well as sitting together at group sessions. We were both locked up in the psych ward for trying to kill ourselves, so we shared a common bond.

During our leisure time, Joseph would usually bring his chessboard with him. He really was quite good at the game (I never beat him—not once. *Grrrr . . .*). We shared our life stories with each other while we were playing and got to know each other pretty well over the next few weeks. By then our talks began to meander into philosophy, politics, religion, and well, anything that happened to be on our minds. I felt that we were becoming friends and hoped that we would stay in touch after we got out of the hospital.

Sleeping was pretty hard for me. I would lie in my steel-framed bed—constructed in such a way that you couldn't hang yourself from it—and stare at the ceiling, wondering what life had in store for me when I got out. Even in the psych ward, I still had a vague belief that God would help me out of this mess I'd gotten myself into. I believe he did help me at various times over the years, although I'm hard pressed to come up with any specific examples.

That was about the extent of my faith through most of my adult years. I guess you could say I was an opportunistic believer. Like, I would occasionally pray to God when I was in trouble or needed something, but we didn't really hang out together much.

Chapter Four

Six weeks after Joseph and I met, we found out that we were both being discharged the next morning. I guess they figured that our heads were suitably shrunk. Joseph and I planned to meet up for breakfast as we usually did and then say our good-byes. I was planning on getting his phone number and maybe even his address so I could look him up after we go out. I was pretty sure he would want to stay in touch too, so I neatly prepared a three-by-five-inch index card with my name, phone number, and address written on it.

And that's when it happened.

Over our last breakfast together, we shared our personal information so that we could get together and continue our friendship on the outside.

So there we were, sitting together and eating our powdered eggs and dry toast, when I decided to ask him something I hadn't really thought of before. He had told me when we first met that he was doing in-between jobs and was meeting with a social worker who would help him find a job. That's why, he said, he was in a bad state of depression and decided to end it all.

I decided to try and set up a time when we could get together. "Maybe tomorrow?" I asked him.

"No," he answered, "I'll be job hunting for the next few days."

That didn't surprise me much, but the next thing he said *did*.

I was just about to shovel a forkful of powdered eggs into my mouth when Joseph leaned over the table toward me and said in a whisper, "I have to tell you something before we leave this place."

I stared back at him, wondering what could be so important to tell me as we were just about out of there.

He leaned in even closer and whispered to me, "I am an angel of the Lord."

I started choking and splattering powdered eggs everywhere. After a few slaps on my back from the nurse on duty, I stopped choking and nodded that I was okay.

I put my chair upright and gingerly sat myself down again across from Joseph, who was frozen in place with eyes wide. I waited until we were alone again. I stared at him and said, "What did you say?"

He looked down at his tray and then lifted his head and looked me in the eye. He started to whisper to me again, "I am an angel."

"Yeah, yeah, I heard that part, Joe. But you must be," I was going to say "crazy," but I caught myself and finished by saying, "confused."

I immediately regretted saying that when I noticed the hurt look in his eyes.

"Sorry, Joe. I just figured you were joking around or something."

"No," he said, with a strained look on his face, "I'm serious. God sent me here to tell you that he had chosen you to interview his son, Jesus Christ."

"Holy shit!" I thought to myself. "What kind of meds is this guy on, *for chrissake*?" I lowered my head and whispered back to him, "I interview Jesus Christ? I don't get it. Why me?"

He looked at me with his bloodshot eyes half-closed and said, "I don't know. I'm just the messenger."

I decided to play along. "When is this supposed to happen?" I thought it best to humor him at this point.

"This Friday. We'll be at your apartment by nine a.m., and we have to leave by nine a.m. on Saturday. Twenty-four hours."

I decided the safest thing to do would be to pretend I was taking him seriously. I thought I was really getting to know Joseph, and then he sprang *this* on me?

"Well, okay then," I lied. "I guess I'll see you and . . . God's son, on Friday. But *for chrissake,* Joseph, why are you just telling me this *now*?"

"I forgot." And with that he picked up his tray and walked out of the dining room.

Chapter Five

By 10:00 a.m. I had packed up all my stuff and was resting in my room when my nurse came in and asked, "You ready to go?" Within an hour I was checked out of the psych ward with a list of my next three psychiatric appointments. My girlfriend Sylvie was parked near the entrance of the hospital. I was pretty bummed out about what Joseph had said to me at breakfast, but I put on my game face.

"Hey, babe! Thanks for picking me up."

I got in the car, leaned over, and kissed Sylvie long and hard. God, I had missed her! We'd seen each other only in supervised visits since I'd been locked up. I could hardly wait to get back to our apartment.

We made small talk on the short trip home, all the while me thinking about what Joseph had said. Really? I was going to interview Jesus Christ, the so-called Son of God? I didn't even know if God really *had* a son. I had pretty much come to the conclusion that Joseph must have been off his meds, but it was Wednesday, and he did say that he'd be bringing God's Son to our apartment on Friday morning. What if he was serious? How *could* he be serious? But what if he *was*? I was starting to think that *I* was the one who was batshit crazy.

It was a short ride home. After I got unpacked, took a shower, made love to Sylvie, and took Poppy out for a pee, my head was about to explode. I told Sylvie I was going to lie down for a while. I needed to think.

Alone in our bedroom, I thought, "Okay, this is stupid. There's no way that Joseph is really an angel of the Lord, so there's no way that Jesus Christ is actually going to physically show up at our apartment door on Friday morning, walk in, and expect me to ask him questions. There is just *no way* that this will happen." I was beside myself.

I couldn't sleep a wink that night, so I decided to—why not? I decided to take Pascal up on his wager and at least *pretend* that maybe I really was going to interview the guy. I started thinking about what I would call him. Jesus Christ? No, too formal. Jesus? Hey, dude?

I began by thinking about what I would ask him if I ever had the chance to really talk to him. The first question that popped into my mind was, "Are you *real*, or am I truly screwed up?"

Okay, so I imagined that he was real, just to play out the imaginary scenario.

The question that next came to mind was, "Why are we here? Not *you*," I said to imaginary Jesus, "but us human beings. What does all this *mean*?"

I quickly began thinking of other questions I would ask him: What is God like? Are *you* God? What happens after we die? Was your mom really a virgin? Two hours later I had quite a list of questions. Here I was just out of the psych ward and thinking of questions I would ask Jesus Christ if I ever met him. What would happen if anyone knew what I was thinking?

"Would I get my old room back?" I wondered.

Joseph and, well, whoever he was bringing with him were supposed to arrive at my apartment by nine o'clock this morning. Why was Joseph doing this? I had no idea what to expect as far as what was going to happen or how they were getting here; put it this way, my mind was in freak mode. I was now convinced that Joseph was a bona fide nutcase, but—but what? I couldn't shake this ominous feeling that he actually might show up with someone claiming to be Jesus Christ. Was he going to hire an actor to play him, or maybe a friend? I was pretty sure that the whole thing was a big joke, being orchestrated by Joseph. Why he would do this was beyond me.

When I hopped out of bed on Friday morning, the first thing I did was put the coffee on and take Poppy out for a pee. Twenty minutes later, I was sitting down at the kitchen table with a cup of strong black coffee.

Sylvie was visiting her mom in Montreal. She wasn't too thrilled when I told her that she would have to vacate the place for a couple of days. I convinced her that her mom needed her to visit. I knew Sylvie's mom hadn't been feeling well and that Sylvie was worried about her. Whatever, it worked.

I nibbled on a piece of toast and had a few sips of coffee when, at 8:55 a.m., there was a knock on my apartment door. *Really*? Was this really happening? My mind was racing. I decided to look through the peephole first just to get a quick glimpse of whoever was out there before I actually opened the door.

I was a bit disappointed to see the toothless visage of Joseph, who was supposed to bring Jesus Christ with him. "Well," I thought, "he's probably here to let me in on the joke."

I slowly opened the door. Joseph walked right in, took a look around, and said, "You need to upgrade." Granted, I lived in an old twelve-story high-rise, but it was my sanctuary.

Poppy quickly worked her way into the picture. She always goes nuts when someone is at the door, and sure enough, she came scampering out of the bedroom, barking like there was no tomorrow. I had learned over the years not to even try and stop her, because then you would have her barking and me screaming at her to stop. When Sylvie was around, she would start yelling too, and then it would turn into a scene from some Adam Sandler movie.

So Joseph is standing there helplessly as Poppy went about humping his leg (she's a sexually confused dog), while I was sitting there waiting for things to settle down, which they eventually did. Poppy's not a big dog; she's mostly a Jack Russell with some other stuff thrown in, but she can make a scene when she wants to. After she settled down and Joseph gently shook her off his leg, he turned to face me.

"I'm really glad to see you, Rog. I hope you're not upset that I forgot to tell you about this until the last minute."

I was glad to see him too.

"Yeah, I'm happy to see you too, Joe. But I'm still pretty confused about this whole situation. I thought you said you were bringing Jesus Christ to my apartment."

"I did." He shrugged.

Chapter Six

Omigod! Someone else was in my apartment! I slowly turned around, and there seated on the couch was . . . was . . . some dude in blue jeans, a black V-neck T-shirt, a neatly trimmed goatee, and a haircut that looked like he went to First Cuts. He appeared to be around thirty or so, and he kind of reminded me of Bruce Springsteen on the album cover of *The Wild, the Innocent and the E Street Shuffle.*

His eyes were dark brown and sparkling. I couldn't help but just stare at him, mouth agape. He looked at me with a kind of wry smile on his face and said, "Hi, Rog. Nice place you've got here. Thanks for having me over."

I know my mouth was open and my jaw was moving, but no words were coming out.

The guy on the couch stood up and started to come toward me. Did he want to shake hands? Hug me? Give me a high five? I just stared at him dumbly as he approached me and reached out his hand for a power grip. I took it as he leaned in and gave me a shoulder bump.

After a few seconds, I took a step back and stared at him. He looked back at me with a big smile, eyes sparkling. No halo around his head, but he had a body that he seemed to take care of. No overhanging belly, and pretty strong looking, to be honest.

I, in comparison, was a slug.

"Okay," he said, "how do you want to do this? Do you have any coffee on the go? Tea? Wine? Anything?"

Hmmm . . . just after nine o'clock in the morning, and he's asking about wine? Oh, well, what the heck. He probably couldn't get drunk anyway if he really was Jesus Christ.

"Yes, actually, I can," he said, apparently reading my mind. "Although the only time I really got drunk was when I heard the news that my cousin John the Baptist had been beheaded. That almost killed me. And the next day, I must admit, I felt like death warmed over," he said with a chuckle.

Okay, so a couple of things were happening there. First, it seemed like he could read my mind, which was kind of creepy when you thought about it. Second, Jesus Christ got drunk when he was on earth? Most Christians I knew weren't going to like that. Some would, I guessed, but most wouldn't.

I finally found my voice. "Uh, do you want some coffee? I just made a fresh pot."

Hmmm . . . well, at least he hadn't asked if I had any pot. I was really scrambling at this point. I mean, can you imagine? What would you do if some guy claiming to be Jesus Christ came to *your* house? Would you offer him something to drink or eat? Did he even *need* to eat or drink?

"No, I don't, but I sure *enjoy* eating and drinking," he said.

I stared at him for a second, trying to figure out what he meant.

I gave my head a shake and said, "Coffee?"

"Yeah, two creams and lots of sugar."

"Must be nice not to have to worry about your health anymore," I thought to myself.

"It is," he said, as if he was in my head. "But I do know what it's like to worry about stuff like that. When I was here back in the day, I actually had to pay attention to my body. Not anymore, though—thank God." He grinned and made a haphazard sign of the cross.

I motioned to the kitchen table, where I had my pages of questions and my computer. He pulled out one of the chairs and plopped himself down. I took my place in front of my computer.

"Do you mind if I smoke?" I asked nervously. I was smoking a lot ever since I got out of the psych ward.

"Nope. In fact, pass me one of those. It's been a while," he said.

"Hmmm," I thought, "it's been a while?" Shit! He must have heard me thinking.

I passed him a cigarette. He grabbed my lighter and fired it up. After a brief coughing spell, he looked up at me and choked out in a harsh voice, "Like I said, it's been a while."

We sat at the kitchen table in silence for a few minutes, smoking our cigarettes and taking sips of coffee.

Joseph must have started wandering around the apartment, apparently, because he was no longer in sight. Maybe angels could become invisible?

"No, but they can be quite slippery," the guy said. Man, he was starting to creep me out a *lot,* knowing everything I was thinking. Like, how could he read my thoughts unless he really *was* Jesus Christ?

"Do you know everything I'm thinking all the time?" I asked.

"No, but I've learned a lot about human psychology over the years."

"Human psychology?"

"Yeah, it's like, I don't know what you're actually going to *say* or *do* until you actually *say* it or *do* it, but I'm pretty good at figuring out what's going on in people's minds. By the way, was that your first interview question?"

"No," I answered, "but we might as well get to it."

"Okay," he said. "Let's do this."

Chapter Seven

I took a deep breath, gathered up my list of questions, and got ready to plunge in. I figured that if this was all a big joke (which I was starting to doubt), I might as well go along with it. Maybe I'd figure out who this guy was and what he was doing this for.

Before I got to my first question, though, I blurted out in all seriousness, "I really want to say right from the start how surprised I am that God chose me to interview you. What was the thinking behind that?" Okay, so I was patronizing the dude, but I wanted him to at least *think* I was sincere. Uh-oh. Did he hear that?

He looked at me with those sparkling eyes of his and said, "When my Dad and I were discussing the possibility of me being interviewed, we narrowed it down to a few people who we thought would do a good job and ask all the hard questions. Some people we thought about were easy to dismiss, like Reese Witherspoon. I tried to talk him into considering Chris Rock, but he nixed that idea, and we both agreed that it shouldn't be a celebrity or a well-known person. In the end, you came out on top."

Higher in the pecking order than Reese didn't really faze me much, but to think that I had topped Chris Rock was definitely a boost to my wannabe comedian ego.

"I'm stunned, really," I said. "Thank you so much for even considering me. I don't consider myself to be all that religious."

"You're not, and that's one of the reasons we chose you. What we were really looking for was someone who would be honest, especially someone who didn't present himself as if he knew all the answers to life. I mean, I'm sure you'd agree, Rog, that you're kind of rough around the edges, but my Dad and I consider that to be a virtue."

I liked what he was telling me, but a part of me was getting curiouser and curiouser. Like, really? They chose *me*? I had to find out more.

"So how many people did you actually consider?" I asked.

He looked at me with that wry smile of his and said, "It wasn't that big of a challenge, dude. I mean, we're talking about God here. The person we needed had to fit certain criteria, such as being alive at this particular time in history, within a certain age bracket, someone living in the United States because that's where Christianity is such a big deal, with certain qualities and skills such as being able to think outside the box, having an outgoing personality, open to new ideas, open to a belief in God, and having a thick skin—those kinds of things," he concluded.

"Well, guess I fit *some* of those criteria," I admitted.

"Don't sell yourself short, Rog. The main reason we decided on you is that you're always questioning *everything*. Yeah, you can be a pain in the ass at times, but it was important for us to have someone who would be willing to ask the tough questions in order to do what we're trying to do here."

He smiled at me and winked. I looked down, a bit embarrassed.

"So what is it, exactly, that we're trying to do here?" I asked.

"What I'm hoping is that we'll spend the next twenty-four hours talking together about things that matter. What I really want *you* to do is to record our conversations and transcribe them. The end result will be a kind of *memoir* of what happens. I want the account, the memoir, to communicate not only what I have to say at this point in human history but also your own thoughts and feelings and descriptions of everything that happens during the next twenty-four—make it twenty-three hours now. Can you do that for me?" he asked.

I nodded my head and said, "Yeah, I think so. I can promise to give it my best shot."

Having said that, I wondered if he could sense how uneasy I was with what he was asking me to do. Like, was Joseph going to jump out from wherever he was and start laughing at me and telling me what a dope I was for actually believing that I was interviewing Jesus Christ?

"He won't," he said simply, "because I *am*."

A bit dramatic, I thought, but I pressed on. "So why now? It's been over two thousand years since you were actually here on earth. What's the purpose for coming out of the closet now?"

"The basic reason is because what people call Christianity today is so completely distorted from the message I came to spread to the world two thousand years ago. My Dad and I are both just sick and tired of all the crap that gets attached to my name in the twenty-first century, continuing a recurring pattern over the centuries. So we thought it was about time for me to make another appearance and grant an interview that clarified what my message was then and how it applied to people today. And with all the technology available today, our hope is that the audio files from this interview will go viral and get the whole world back on track. So that, basically, is the reason we decided to take this approach."

He hesitated for a second before saying, "What has gone on in my name over the past two thousand years, and it continues today, is unconscionable. Millions of lives over the centuries have been ruined, even ended, by the Christian Church. Christians have engaged in the worst atrocities and barbarisms imaginable, *and all in my name*! More Christians have been tortured and murdered over the centuries *by other Christians* than all other religions and ideologies combined. I came here two thousand years ago to proclaim the dawning of a new age and a new way of thinking and living, which I called the Kingdom of God. That message has been lost as Christianity developed over the centuries. That's why God sent me here today, to let the whole world know what *really* happened and what I *really* taught while I was here back in the day."

His eyes bored into mine. "So, Rog, are you ready to do this?" he asked.

"Yes," I answered solemnly, "I'm ready."

But before getting started, I decided to let the cat out of the bag.

"First, though, to be honest, I'm still not sure if you are who you say you are," I said.

He laughed out loud and said, "I know, Rog. I realize how difficult this is for you. Let me say it plainly: God, my Father and your Father, appointed me to be his messenger when my cousin John baptized me in the Jordan River all those years ago. That's when he adopted me to be his son. At this point I'm just hoping that you'll give me the benefit of the doubt."

"Okay, man, no one has popped out of the woodwork yet, so I'll keep an open mind. I'm just really confused right now. I don't even know what to call you. Like, the name Jesus seems so archaic. Is it okay if I call you Joshua? Josh even?"

He looked a bit surprised. Didn't he know I was going to ask him that?

"Yeah, sure," he said. "Around the world I'm known by lots of different names. I don't pay much attention to what I'm called, really. I like to look into a person's heart and see what the underlying motivation is." He looked down, for a few seconds, at the numerous cigarette burns on the kitchen table and then said, "I was named Yeshua in my mother tongue, Aramaic. Yeshua was a common name in first-century Palestine, something like, as you're suggesting, Joshua. But through the centuries, my name was eventually translated into Jesus, at least in English. Nowadays most English-speaking people seem to think that Jesus is a special name reserved just for me. But it isn't. So, yeah, Joshua or Josh is fine with me."

"Okay, then . . . Josh," I said.

"Cool," he responded.

Chapter Eight

Time to get started, I figured. I turned on the recording device on my computer and looked down at my neatly prepared questions.

I decided to go with the first question I had thought of when I started preparing for this interview.

"I want to ask what most people in my circle of family and friends think of as *the* basic question about life, and that is, why are we here? On earth, that is."

I could see him kind of pondering the question, although I was pretty sure he knew the answer. His eyes were closed, and his head kind of hanging down.

He slowly raised his head, opened his eyes, and said, "Good question. Good question."

"Okay," I thought, "so he thinks it's a good question. Well, good for me. We are at least starting off on the same page."

Joshua was staring at me intently. He said, "It's important to understand, first, that God *loves* to create. In fact, I would go further and say he *has* to create. It's just a big part of who he is. He has a purpose for everything he creates. So for you guys—humans, that is—he created the *conditions* for self-conscious beings to evolve here on this planet. Now he's waiting to see how you're going to continue to evolve. You matter to him. I don't know how else to put it."

"Okay, I get that, but you haven't really answered my question. What's the reason for us *being* here on earth?"

He paused, closed his eyes, and said, "You're here on earth to *be*, to be the kind of person you know you can be—the kind of person you *want* to be. To do that you need to live in the present, in the *now*. You're here to learn how to live a life without fear or anxiety or guilt or regrets, trusting God for everything and treating other people the way you want to be treated. You're here to learn how to love *extravagantly*, to be compassionate and forgiving toward others, to be generous with your time and money, and to stand up and speak out against injustice wherever you see it, helping those less fortunate than you and always looking for the good in other people."

I was nonplussed. Something was missing.

"I get what you're saying, Josh, but you're not saying anything about *why* we're here; you're just saying how we should live once we *are* here. I live with so many regrets and the consequences of bad decisions that have screwed up my life that I can't honestly say that I enjoy it much at all. I mean, it wasn't all that long ago that I tried to kill myself."

"*Hmmm*"—he sighed—"okay, Rog, how about this: What do *you* want out of life? What gives *your* life meaning? What makes *you* happy? People constantly strive for pleasure, wealth, power, and prestige—all in an attempt to find meaning and purpose in their lives. What's the *point*? If you believe that the universe is cold and uncaring, what possible purpose does one have for valuing one's existence? Maybe you're hoping to leave a positive legacy for your children and grandchildren or leave the world a slightly better place because you existed. But who cares? The universe doesn't care; it's merely a cold, meaningless entity. The truth of the matter is that only *you* can determine what the meaning of your life is. You discover the meaning of your life by looking *within*. The meaning of life is up to *you* to decide. Now use your power of reason to figure it out."

"So the meaning of life is up to *me* to figure out? What about . . . like . . . how . . ." Oh, well, whatever. I didn't get it. I quickly recovered. "But doesn't God already know what meaning I'm going to attach to my life and experiences?"

"No, he doesn't. God doesn't know everything in the way most people think he does. Here's how it works: *God knows everything that can be known*. But he's not omniscient. People *think* he is, but he's not. He has ideas and even a few plans for certain things that happen on earth, but he doesn't know what hasn't happened yet. He loves everything he creates; he just doesn't know what the final outcome will be when intelligent self-conscious beings evolve, both here on earth and on millions of other planets in the universe. That's part of the fun of being God."

"So how does what you're telling me relate to the meaning of life?" I asked.

"Well, think about it. What do *you* think is the meaning of life?" He was looking right into my eyes when he asked. It was unnerving.

"Life," I ventured. "Like, sure, we all have good times and bad times, tragedies and joy, good relationships and bad ones, sometimes just 'bad luck,' and I guess having 'good luck' must go along with that. But why am I *here*? I mean, I heard what you just said about trusting God and being kind to others and all that stuff, but you still haven't answered the question 'Why?' Why did God create us in the first place? If I knew the answer to that, I think that would go a long way to explaining the meaning of life and helping us human types to get through it."

"The short answer is that God didn't *create* you, at least not directly. He created the *conditions* for the evolution of self-conscious beings here on earth. Human beings evolved into self-conscious beings just as God eventually evolved into a self-conscious being. Humans are very much like God in that respect. Consciousness cannot cease to be consciousness; once it exists, it cannot *not* exist."

"So you're saying that human beings, like God, cannot cease to exist? If that's true, that would take a lot of anxiety and fear away from the thought of dying."

"It *is* true. That's what I kept telling people when I was here back in the day. There's no need to worry about what happens after you die. Life continues. God wants everyone to enjoy *this* life now, always being in the present, and to trust him for everything. That was the message I proclaimed: the Kingdom of God is *here*—right here, right now. My message about the Kingdom of God had nothing to do with what happened after you died. This life on earth is meant to provide you with the opportunity to learn to live life to the fullest and to become the kind of person you know you can be."

"But why did God even start the big bang in the first place? Was he just bored of being alone in the universe or what?"

Joshua looked at me as if I had sprouted horns. Was my question too far out in left field? I didn't think so, but Joshua looked puzzled.

"Before time and space existed, what you humans call God was in a kind of deep sleep. He eventually woke up, wiped the cobwebs from his eyes, and realized that he could do things, like thinking, and that he was aware of himself and the nothingness that surrounded him. Then he realized that he could make something, anything, appear just by thinking about it. So he thought about how cool it would be to make stuff, and *voilà*, he put the whole universe in motion with, well, with a big bang. I'm not sure how else to put it."

"It sounds to me like you're leaving a lot of stuff out of that story. Can you fill in some of the details? Like, what do you mean that God was in a deep sleep?"

"Look, Rog, I'm just trying to give you a hint of what happened before time and space existed, using words and language that cannot possibly even begin to describe what happened. We'll just have to leave it like that for now."

I thought about that for a second and then asked, "So how are we supposed to know *anything* about why we're here?"

"You have to use your minds, your *reason*. You guys have evolved into beings with beautiful minds. True, many humans are just part of the bewildered herd, so to speak, and don't pay much attention to learning or developing their minds. I'm not saying humans are stupid, but—well, I guess I *am* saying that. But my point is that nobody *has* to be stupid. You all have self-conscious minds and freedom, so you can decide for yourselves if you want to remain ignorant about life or if you want to explore and be open to whatever. All truth is God's truth, so you don't have to be afraid of it. So many Christians are afraid of science, for example, because they think that there might be a scientific truth that goes against what they already believe. Why be afraid of the truth?" he asked rhetorically.

"Well, 'ignorance is bliss,' as the saying goes," I said.

"And that's for each individual to decide, Rog. If you want to be ignorant in this life, go for it. But if you're curious to explore this world of wonder and keep an open mind to whatever you may find, well, that's what God created your minds for—not to atrophy but to be excited and stimulated and *used*. That's the key element in the Kingdom of God message I proclaimed so many years ago. *That's* why you guys are here—to live life to the fullest every day, encouraging others and experiencing everything God has created."

Man, this guy was talking like he really knew this stuff to be true. Still, I couldn't help but ask, "But what's the point of having to live here on this planet for such a relatively short time? Millions die before they're even five years old, *for chrissake*! Couldn't God have made it so that we were just born into his Kingdom right from the beginning without having to go through all *this*?"

Joshua looked down at the table, picked up his coffee cup, and took a sip. He said, "My message of the Kingdom of God was about *this* life here on earth—how to live your life to the fullest every day and to show compassion toward others, being generous with your time and money, speaking out against injustice, helping those less fortunate than you, and trusting God for all your needs. You start your journey here on earth when you take your first breath: a journey of becoming *aware* of who you are, who God is, and to think more and more like God thinks through your experiences, choices, hardships, disabilities, relationships—through everything you go through here. It's all part of your *becoming* the kind of person you know you can be. It's God's nature to *create*, just as it is *your* nature as self-conscious human beings to create: your children, ideas, music, books, art, technologies, and ultimately, your own meaning for being here. And, of course, because he wanted people to hang out with and enjoy the whole universe with."

"What about those who die when they're kids or are born with horrible birth defects or who turn out to be psychopaths or—"

"Whoa, hold on, Rog. We'll get to that when the time is right. All you need to know at this point is this: it is what it is."

"Hmmm," I thought, "the old 'it is what it is' line. Maybe he just didn't really know—"

"I *do* know, dude, but we're not there yet."

I felt like I was getting lost right from the start. Here I was talking with a guy claiming to be Jesus Christ, and I was already scrambling to figure out his response to my first question.

I decided to ask him something that would really show whether or not he is who he says he is.

"Okay, man, let's try this: What does God *expect* of us human beings?" Not a great question, really, but like I said, I was scrambling.

He didn't miss a beat.

"God loves you and all human beings without any conditions. He wants everyone to be happy and at peace with him, with oneself, and with other people, regardless of one's religion or one's personal circumstances in this life. But he doesn't *need* anything. He doesn't *need* your worship; he doesn't have a *need* to judge you or to punish you or to condemn you. What God *wants* is for human beings to have an *awareness* of him, intelligent creatures to astonish and to live forever together. He wants you to be happy and to enjoy your lives here on earth."

"Yeah, okay, I know *I* want to be happy and to enjoy this life, but, you know, sometimes I do and sometimes I don't."

"Right, it depends. Mostly it depends on two things: we all want to be cool, and we all want to be liked."

I stared at him as if *he* had sprouted horns. "Cool and liked? So you're saying that, to be happy and to enjoy this life, you have to be cool and liked?"

"Well, think about it. Don't you want to be cool and liked?"

"I'm not sure what you mean, dude."

"I'll tell you this: God wants to be cool and liked, and if you're evolving into an image of God, it just makes sense that you want the same thing as he does."

"So God wants to be cool and liked?"

"He *is* cool, and he very much wants to be liked. But, you know, some people do and some don't."

"So, that's it? That's the meaning of life?"

"That's about it."

I immediately regretted thinking, "Geez, Monty Python did a better job of explaining—"

"You think?" he said with a bit of a hurt look on his face.

Man, this mind-reading thing could get real old, real fast.

Chapter Nine

I wanted to get the *big picture* from him before we started getting into the details. "I want to get right down to it and ask you some questions about what God is really like."

Joshua pondered my question for a moment and then said, "Yeah, I do love talking about my Dad, and he is the reason for me being here today. Remember, he's *your* God and *your* Dad too. All human beings are children of God."

I felt a bit embarrassed when he said that, but he was right. I did believe that we are all children of God. Whether or not we're *aware* of that fact and live as children of God is up to each individual, I figured.

"God has always been and always will be. I know that's a tough concept for the human mind to grasp, but lots of things that happen to you guys here on earth aren't clearly understood, or understood at all. He basically just put things in motion during the creation of the universe and then stood back to see what was going to happen."

I slowly rose from the table and took a few steps into the living room, thinking about the implications of what he was saying. I always think more clearly when I'm walking around (especially when I'm talking on the telephone). Finally I asked, "So how personally involved *is* God with human beings here on earth?"

"Well, most Christians believe that *everything* that happens to them is so important to God that it *must* be him causing it: deciding who lives and who dies, who gets hurt and who doesn't, who is born where and what their upbringing is like—that sort of thing. That's just not how it works. Some things, like nature, are set in motion, and God takes a pretty much hands-off approach to it. God's a lot less 'hands-on' than most Christians think. He *does* want intimacy with human beings, but most Christians have taken it *way* too far. Most Christians believe that God is concerned with the smallest details of their lives. Let me ask you this, Rog: When you have the flu, do you pray that God will heal you?"

"Well, yeah," I said.

"And does he?"

"Well, I like to think that prayer helps me get better faster."

"Really, Rog? You really believe that?"

"No," I admitted.

"Now we're getting somewhere. Like when your friend Richard dove into that river and floated up paralyzed from the neck down for life, was that God who did that? Or was it because Richard was drinking or had bad luck or whatever? I'll tell you this: God didn't paralyze him. Life is just like that. God is not causing every little thing to happen in every human life. He does, however, want intimacy, a sense of being *one*, with every human being. Remember how I taught my disciples to pray?"

"Uh, yeah, something along the lines of it's good to pray?" I asked, not having a clue what he meant.

"I taught them to talk to God using the term 'abba.' 'Abba' is an Aramaic word that means 'dad' or 'daddy.' It's a term that implies intimacy and affection. I used it all the time when I was meditating. When I was about to be arrested and crucified, I said to God, 'Abba, please don't make me do this. I don't want to die.' But that term, 'abba,' gives you an idea how intimate we were. And that's what I wanted for all my followers: to have a profound *awareness* of God."

I slowly rose from the table and took a few steps into the living room, thinking about the implications of what he was saying.

"Remember the time when your daughter Daisy was five years old and playing with friends on the swings at the park? When she fell from the swing and broke her arm, did you *want* her to break her arm? Did you *cause* her to break her arm? Did you *know* that she was going to fall from the swing and break her arm?"

"No, no, and no. I felt *so bad* that I had taken my eyes off her, even for a moment. I feel like I learned a lesson that day."

"Yes, you did. Accidents happen, often times a lot more serious than a broken arm. When accidents happen, no matter how simple or tragic, God is there. He doesn't *cause* things to happen. Accidents are accidents. But he's there. You make decisions, and with every decision you make, there are consequences. It's like when someone decides to live in that part of the United States known as Tornado Alley. When a house or a town is destroyed by a tornado and some people are killed and maimed, was that God who did that?"

"No?" I asked hesitantly.

"No, that's not how it works. If you decide to build your house in Tornado Alley, you have to expect the occasional tornado to pass by and destroy buildings and hurt people. But to listen to Christians who survive a tornado talk, you'd think that God sent the tornado as some kind of—some kind of what? Test? To show how powerful he is? No. Nature is one of those things that he set in motion, but he doesn't pay much attention to it, unless he has a good reason to. But back to tornado survivors, what do you hear? 'Oh, thank God that he spared us! He loves us so much that he protected our whole family!' Of course, the people next door were all killed, but *they* survived, so it *must* have been God protecting them. And anyway, the family next door was Muslim, so obviously God was punishing them for being Muslim."

I was starting to feel uncomfortable. "This is getting pretty deep," I said.

"*Life* is deep—and difficult. At times it can be exciting and cool, while at other times, you can hardly drag your sorry ass out of bed. Have faith in God. Love others in your life and learn to be compassionate and forgiving toward everyone. Then you will understand what it means to live life to the fullest. The message I brought two thousand years ago is that the Kingdom of God is *within* you. Now bring it *out* and *live* it. Live your life to the fullest every day. My message is still the same today as it was back in the day: the Kingdom of God can be accessed right here, right now. God made it all for you."

"You mean the whole humans-on-earth thing?" I asked.

"I mean *the whole fucking universe*!"

I was impressed with his passion. Still, I couldn't help but ask, "So how does what you're saying relate to what God is *like*?"

"It's all about knowing yourself. Know yourself, and you will know what God is like and why you're here on earth. Look deep within. What kind of person are you? What kind of person do you want to be? You can't just pick and choose with this stuff. Either we're reflections of God's image or we're not. The incredible order and design we see in the universe and on this planet, along with the intricacy and complexity of DNA, should lead any reasonable person to come to the conclusion that there must be intelligence behind it all. But, you know, some do and some don't."

"Listening to you talk about the whole creation thing a moment ago, it sounds like God did a lot of experimenting with his creation," I ventured.

"I wouldn't use that term, but—"

"What term would you use, then?" I asked.

"Okay, he *experimented*. But by saying that I mean that God started it all and watches it all happen. The thing with doing that is that you just never know what's going to happen. God *thought* he knew, but it turned out that he didn't."

"Really? God didn't know how things would turn out with people here on earth?" I asked.

"It's not *Star Wars*, Rog. Life doesn't follow a Hollywood script. It bears keeping in mind, too, that self-conscious, intelligent life has evolved on millions of planets in the universe over billions of years. You'll find out more about the universe someday, but for now I'm just concerned with you guys on this planet."

"So you talk about God as if he's a person, like when you call him your 'Dad,' and that God wants to have a 'relationship' with human beings. So, is he a person?"

"No. The concept of a God who lives somewhere in the sky and intervenes in the lives of human beings developed when humans evolved from conscious mammals into self-conscious sapiens, when awareness evolved into self-awareness. The first humans who developed self-consciousness were eventually capable of understanding concepts such as time and mortality. Humans evolved to where they could understand the difference between 'past' and 'future,' and that they would eventually die. They didn't know what it *meant* to 'die,' but they began to notice that fellow humans who could walk and talk and use tools and hunt together one day would suddenly stop doing those things and lie inert and unmoving on the ground the next day. What happened? It was at that point in the evolutionary cycle that the concept of a being superior to humans began to take hold. The hope developed among these first self-conscious humans that this superior being might be the key to understanding mortality and the meaning of it. It's one thing to die, but it's quite another to know you're *going* to die. That raised all sorts of questions in the developing human mind, which you guys are still trying to figure out over one hundred thousand years later, since humans first evolved into self-conscious beings. I'm telling you something that most humans only find out about after they die, Rog. I know it's hard, but I need you to stay with me here."

"Okay, Josh, so how should we humans *think* about God?"

"God is *life itself*. God is what animates all living things in the universe. Take your own human body as an example. You don't use batteries, and you don't plug in at night. So what *animates* your body? What makes it *alive*? What you guys call God animates you and all living things. True, I refer to God as a person, my Father, because I myself am limited by language and culture. But I came to the realization that God was not a person but a *spirit*. Human beings are confined by language and thought, as I was back in the day. But God is beyond language, beyond thinking. He is *life itself*."

"So like God is a kind of *life force*?" I was starting to feel very anxious about what he was telling me.

"No. God *is* life. I don't know how else to say it. God is *life*, God is *love*. God animates everything that breathes. But the only way humans can even begin to conceive of the inconceivable is with human language. So humans can talk about how God loves and cares for all human beings and all intelligent life in the universe, but until humans evolve further, you guys are bound by language and thought to conceive of God as a person like you are. So we talk about where this superior being 'lives' and how we can secure this being's favor and blessing. But such thinking about God is embarrassing to the modern twenty-first-century person.

We know now that God does not live in the sky. We know now that the scope of the universe is beyond human comprehension. Archaic, Bronze Age thinking about God and the universe merely acts as a barrier to scientific exploration and progressive thinking in the modern world."

"I'm starting to get it now. We can't talk about God in real terms within the confines of language, so we do the best we can with our current state of language and thinking."

"Yep. We do the best we can with what we have and know at this point in human evolution. There is no god who lives in the sky and keeps record books so that he can punish or reward you on the basis of your behavior 'down here' on earth. You guys now know that you live in an ordered world with mathematically precise natural laws that govern the universe. Yet for some strange reason, the vast majority of human beings continue to believe in magic, superstition, miracles, and fairy tales. It's time to grow up."

We looked at each other as if to agree that it was time to move on.

Chapter Ten

I didn't really think it was a hoax anymore, not with this guy sitting at my kitchen table with the sparkling eyes, able to discern what I was thinking, and saying the things he was saying with such—authority.

I looked up at him and said, "I just need a few minutes, Josh. I'll be back in a jiff."

I got up and made my way into my bedroom. There was Joseph lying on the bed and watching TV. Netflix, I think. At a quick glance, I noticed that he was watching a show about zombies. *Fast* zombies. Like zombies on crack. I guess I was a bit surprised to find him watching TV while we were talking at my kitchen table. I decided to ask Joshua if Joseph could join us. We had become pretty close friends in the psych ward, and I wanted him to be included in the interview too.

I turned around and went to the bathroom to splash some cold water on my face. I was feeling dizzy. The whole situation was just too surreal. Was I really sitting at my kitchen table with Jesus Christ? If so, I figured that I had to rethink my whole belief system, which shouldn't be too hard, actually. I didn't know *what* I believed before this interview was sprung on me. Okay, a quick inventory. I believed that God existed; I was pretty much convinced of that. And here I was talking with a guy who claimed to be Jesus Christ. Then the thought hit me: I've done a *lot* of drugs in my life; could this be some sort of drug-induced hallucination? Possibly, possibly. Was I just losing it mentally? The two seemed to go hand in hand.

I came back to the kitchen table and said, “Ready to continue?” “Giddyup,” he answered.

Chapter Eleven

As I glanced at my notes, I noticed Joseph had come out of the bedroom and was sitting quietly on the couch. He looked sheepishly at Joshua, obviously wanting to sit with us as the interview continued.

"For sure, Joe," Joshua said. "I think it's best if you hang with us for the rest of the way."

Joseph smiled with relief and settled in at the kitchen table.

I smiled at Joseph as he pulled out a chair at the back of the table. I felt a twinge of guilt seeing him sitting there, although now he had a big smile on his face and his eyes were gleaming. Looking at him reminded me of the time we first met and the talks and escapades we had together while in the psych ward. I wished I had the time to interview Joseph for a while. He had had such a positive effect on me when I was so down in the dumps after trying to kill myself. He always seemed in a good mood, and it was contagious.

Joseph sneaked a glance at me and continued smiling. I felt entirely comfortable with Joseph listening in. I wondered if I would ever see him again in this life after today.

It's funny, but as I looked back on the whole experience with Joseph in the psych ward and now with him hanging out with us, I believed that he was actually an angel of the Lord. But to me he was just Joe. It seemed to me that all Joseph wanted to do was to please the Lord.

"I could learn from that," I thought.

Chapter Twelve

I looked down at my notes and said, "Are you ready to talk about *yourself* for a bit, Josh?"

Joshua hesitated before answering, as if he was weighing his next words.

"Yeah, sure," he said.

"*Hmmm,* I guess they don't weigh much," I thought. "Well, how *about* you then? Who *are* you, anyway?" I asked.

He looked right into my eyes. "Go ahead. Ask the big question on your mind right now."

"Okay. Are you *God*?"

"No," he answered.

"*No?*"

"No. There is only one God and Father of us all."

"Most Christians reading this interview aren't going to like that," I ventured.

"What can I say? It is what it is. I realize that me being part of the so-called Trinity, one God with three personalities, is the foundation of orthodox Christian belief throughout the centuries and that most Christians reading this are going to be terribly upset. But look at it from my perspective. How do you think *I* feel about being elevated to godly status when I never claimed to be God? There is but one God, my Father, *our* Father. Some early Christians, led by Paul of Tarsus, distorted that truth about me from the very start. Paul's alleged vision on the road to Damascus led him to believe that I was God. I died physically just like every person eventually dies, but life continues. I continued to exist after my physical death. That's what God wanted to get across to human beings. Your bodies are merely a dwelling place for your consciousness, who you really are. I was chosen by God to communicate that truth in no uncertain terms. As you look at me now, what do you see?"

I thought about that for a moment before saying, "I see a guy sitting at my kitchen table who looks like a human being." Pretty lame response, I know, but . . .

"I *am* a human being! I just have a different kind of body now, just as every human being receives a new, transformed body from God after their earth bodies die. I was chosen by God to be the first human being to show *other* human beings what happened to them after they died. I mean, how cool is that?"

"Pretty damn cool," I said, agreeing. I think I was even getting a bit envious just thinking about it. I would give my left nut to be God's adopted son. Heck, *both* my nuts. Okay, maybe just my left one.

"In the four Gospel accounts written about my life that made it into the Bible, only the gospel with John's name attached to it, which was written eighty years after my death, portrayed me as divine. The idea that I was God wasn't made an official doctrine of Christianity until centuries after my death, and it took all that time, along with lots of pretty intense arguments and infighting among the different Christian factions during those years, to come to the conclusion that I was God. Matthew, Mark, and Luke, authors of the first three gospels, never had me claiming to be God."

I had read about the differences between the first three gospels and the gospel of John before, but here I was actually hearing about it from Jesus Christ himself.

"Like the time on the cross when I prayed, *'My God,* why have you forsaken me?' I thought I was being very clear that I was *not* God. Then in the gospel of Mark, I'm reported as saying, 'I don't know what God has planned for the earth. Only He knows.' And in Matthew I'm quoted as saying, 'There is only one who is good, and that one is God.' I did actually say those things. I was keen on getting the point across that there is only one God and that it's not me."

"I hear you," I said, "but can you imagine how many Christians will get to this point in the interview, slam the book shut, or click off YouTube and accuse me, actually *you*, of being a heretic? I mean, most Christians believe that *you are God*. And you're telling me, and by extension everybody in the world, that you're *not* God. How do you think that will play in the Christian community?" I asked.

"It just goes with the territory, Rog. The whole thing about me being God is, in fact, one of the main reasons God wanted me to do this interview—to set the record straight once and for all. That's why we're doing this."

"Okay, so you're telling me who you're *not*, but you really haven't revealed all that much yet about who you *are*."

Joshua reached for my pack of cigarettes, took out two, and lit one, passing it to me. Then he lit one for himself. He took a big drag, exhaled slowly, and looked intently into my eyes.

"Very simply, I was completely human. I had all the normal human experiences and emotion. I was born and died as a human being. I loved and was loved, and I tried to be kind and compassionate to everyone I interacted with. I also got angry and irritable at times, and upset, and depressed, and fed up with some people, especially the religious leaders of the day. On the flip side of the coin, I experienced joy and happiness and good times. I was human. I tried to be an example of how to live a life focused on God and trusting him for all your needs. I feel like I poured myself out for other people, all because of the love and compassion I had for them."

"So was your mom really a virgin when you were born?"

"No." He laughed. "The whole myth about my mom being a virgin wasn't created until decades after my death, and even then only in the gospels of Matthew and Luke. The gospels written by Mark and John never mention it, nor did Paul in any of his letters. It was part of the legend that began to develop a few decades after I was crucified."

Suddenly, as if a floodgate had opened, other key questions (well, key for me) came to mind.

"If you were completely human, weren't you affected by 'original sin'?"

"There *is* no such thing as 'original sin.' That whole idea has caused so much grief and anguish over the millennia that it makes me sick to my stomach. It's a theological idea that developed centuries after my death, by the religious ruling elite. It was all part of the hysterical intent to keep the faithful under their thumb and to add to their number of followers. That's one of the reasons I'm here talking to you today—to let people know that there are so many falsehoods being foisted on people in my name."

"So what about some of the miraculous stuff they said you did when you were here? Did you really walk on water or turn water into wine?" I asked.

"No. It's all part of the legend that built up around me in the decades after I died. Have you ever seen a human being walk over a swimming pool on a summer day? Me neither. If I really did all the things that people began to say that I did, I wouldn't have been human. It's true that I could heal people of various illnesses, but many, many traditional healers over the past few thousands of years have had that ability. Some human beings are just more tuned in to spiritual reality, and the power that comes with that awareness, than most. The thing to remember is this: anything I did while here back in the day any human being should be able to do. I told my followers that truth many times. I didn't do anything that any human couldn't do, even today. As I told my followers many times while traveling together, 'You will be able to do even *greater* things than I did.' And they did."

"But . . . but," I began. I wasn't sure what to say. What ended up coming out of my mouth was, "Didn't you perform lots of miracles when you were here before?"

"No. Healings are not miracles by definition, and I never did anything that broke any laws of nature, the definition of a 'miracle.' Like, look at what you guys are able to do to heal people today. All it takes is human intelligence, imagination, and technology. Can you imagine what people even fifty years ago, not to mention two thousand years ago, would think about what doctors are able to do today?"

I saw where he was going with this. Yeah, what doctors can do today would be regarded as miracles even in the span of my lifetime.

Joshua continued, "God is not in the miracle business. If someone really could multiply a few loaves of bread and some fish sticks to feed thousands of people, there would be no starvation in the world. I don't know how to say it any plainer: God doesn't do miracles. The closest thing to a miracle I've ever seen is when the Chicago Cubs won the World Series in 2016."

I was a huge Cubs fan, having grown up and still living in Chicago, and it *was* the first time the Cubs won the World Series since 1908, but I didn't see how it broke any physical laws.

"I was joking."

"Oh, yeah, right, well, I figured that, but—"

I thought I'd sneak in a question he might not be expecting.

He already knew where I wanted to go.

"Yes, I was tempted in every way that every human being is, and that every human being has been tempted with since the beginning of human history."

"Tempted in *every* way?"

"Yeah, Rog, in every way. I had to learn to be respectful of beautiful young women and to think of women as equal to men. Yeah, I wondered sometimes what it would be like to be with some of the attractive women who were around, but I did my best to be a gentleman. I was a regular guy in that regard. I got turned on at times, and my imagination would get the better of me sometimes. But I was no 'God in disguise' as so many Christians seem to believe. I had my own doubts and biases and prejudices and temptations. I was human."

"Do you still have doubts and prejudices?"

"No. Now I know things I never even thought about when I was here before. I'll give you an example of what I mean, though. Most of my teaching took place in northern Israel, mostly in the region of Galilee. On one occasion, I ventured into non-Jewish territory, not to preach the good news of the Kingdom of God, at least not yet, but to lie low for a while. While I was there, this Greek woman came to see me and started telling me about how her daughter was sick. She fell at my feet and asked me to heal her daughter. I told her that I had come to proclaim the good news only to my own people, the Jews, which I believed at that time in my life. But the way she responded *made me change my mind*. She basically said that if God loved all people equally and without condition, then the Kingdom of God message was meant for everyone, regardless of religion or race or gender. I knew in my heart right then that I had been wrong to limit God's message to the Jews only. I said to her, 'You're right. Go home to your daughter. She is healed.'

You know what she did? *She challenged my racial prejudice.* It was that incident that moved me to change my mind about what I was doing and to realize that the Kingdom of God message was meant for *all* people. She opened up my thinking, and I learned a new tolerance. It was an important change of mind and heart for me. But you know what it shows? It shows I was human."

I felt humbled. Joshua had cleared up some basic things about who he was. He wasn't God, but he lived his life in daily communion with God, who he called his "Father." He was starting to make me see that God was *my* Father too.

Chapter Thirteen

I got up to pour us each another cup of coffee. Before I sat down, I lit a cigarette and offered one to Joshua. He took it and lit it. "This is so weird actually smoking with Jesus Christ!" I thought. But as I sat down at my place, I couldn't shake the feeling that something wasn't right with this interview.

I couldn't help it. Here I was talking with who I now believed was Jesus Christ, and he was telling me such intimate details about himself and his time here on earth over two thousand years ago.

"I wish I could have been there to *see* you in action back in the day rather than merely talking about it," I said. I already had the sense after just a couple of hours that this whole interview format was not going to cut it. But here we were, and I was committed to making the best of it.

That's when Joshua broke in. "You're right, Rog," he said. "This isn't working exactly as we hoped it would. My Dad and I figured that a simple back-and-forth interview would get the job done—that it was the best way to cut through the crap of what's been going on in my name for the past two millennia so that I could once and for all 'set the record straight.' But it's not going to happen unless we tweak the process."

"Tweak the process?" I repeated. "Okay, Joshua, I have no idea what you're talking about. It seems to me that we're kind of stuck doing this interview. What could you possibly do to 'tweak' it?" I asked.

Joshua thought for a moment and then said, "Here's the thing, Rog: I was talking with God while you were checking on Joseph, and I couldn't help but ask him how we could do a better job of it. He was very clear. He told that, instead of merely *telling* you about stuff, I need to *show* you some things."

"*Show* me some things?" I said. "How the heck are you going to do *that*?" I asked.

Just then Joseph plodded into the living room from my bedroom and plopped himself down on the couch.

"Yeah, Lord, how are you going to do *that*?"

My mind was whirling. Joshua looked over at Joseph and then turned back to me. "Here's what's going to happen," he said. "My Dad and I put our heads together, and we came up with an alternate plan. When we get to places in the interview where I need to *show* you rather than merely *tell* you what happened, we're going to go back and see what really happened."

"*What?*" I thought. "Go back? Go back to *where*?" I had no idea what the heck he was talking about.

"I'm going to take you and Joe back to first-century Palestine during the time I was there two thousand years ago. Some things need to be *experienced* rather than just *told* about," he said.

Joseph struggled to get off the couch (he was not in the same shape as the Son of God, for whatever reason), stood up, and came over to the kitchen table.

"Are you telling me we're going back to when you were here before?" he asked.

"Yes," Joshua said. "That's exactly what we're going to do."

My head exploded (figuratively, of course). I was hearing what Joshua was saying, but I couldn't connect the dots. How the heck were we supposed to go back two thousand years and actually *see* Jesus the Nazarene in action? My thoughts were coming fast and furious. How could Joshua be in the same place as Jesus? What if Jesus of Nazareth saw us—saw *him*? I'd watched tons of science-fiction movies over the years, and all I could think of was, "This could be dangerous. Could we accidentally change history or something? What would happen if Jesus the Nazarene were to recognize Joshua? Like, what if Jesus saw Joshua, being the same person, and Jesus recoiled at the sight of him and flew into a panic or . . . or . . . or what?" I couldn't begin to comprehend where Joshua was going with this. "What if—"

Joshua cut into my thoughts. "Not to worry, Rog," he said. "God has it all figured out."

Joseph jumped back into the fray. "Look, Lord, I've been around a long time, and you've never done anything like this before. The human is right; what if something happens that changes something? What if you recognize yourself?"

Recognize himself? This was getting very confusing. I was just getting comfortable with the interview setting, and now Joshua wanted to take us back into the past? I started to get a really bad feeling in the pit of my stomach. I couldn't shake the thought that the potential for something really bad to happen was certainly possible, at least according to my human way of thinking.

Joshua heard me, of course, and said, "It's okay, Rog. Well, I guess what I mean is that *I* don't have to worry. I've never done this before, but I'm pretty sure my Dad and I have it pretty well figured out. It's the best way for me to really show you what I'm trying to tell you." Then he added, "It could be a bit dangerous for *you*, though."

Dangerous for *me*? What the heck? Which is exactly what I asked him.

"What the, Josh? It could be dangerous for *me* but not *you*? What about Joseph?" I asked.

"No," he said, "Joseph's cool. He's an angel, so he can't be killed or physically hurt."

"Can't be killed or physically hurt?" I thought. "But what about *me*?" I asked, terrified at what he was going to say.

"It's not about *you*, Rog. I mean, I love you and all that stuff, but the risk is minimal."

"Minimal?" I asked with eyes wide.

He said, "Like I just said, I've never done this before, so of course there's going to be some risk to you, but hey, you like adventure, right?"

"I like adventure when I have some control over what happens," I responded. "But this situation sounds like a recipe for disaster."

Joseph decided to put in his two cents worth, "What's the problem? Remember whom you're talking to. You think the Son of God is going to let anything bad happen to you?"

Joseph looked over at Joshua, and Joshua met his eyes. Joshua had one eyebrow raised as if to say, "I've got this one."

So I thought—no, I actually *said,* "What's the worst that could happen to me? How about dying? Or worse, ending up in a wheelchair for the rest of my life?"

Joshua came back at me, "Yeah, both are possibilities, but I thought you'd be the last one to worry about what might happen. I mean, let's face it, Rog, you have a lot more past than future."

I was getting totally bummed out about the whole thing, but I decided he was right. Like, it wasn't all that long ago that I tried to orchestrate my own final exit, so what's the big deal if I die? I just didn't want to be horribly maimed, though. I'd rather die, as long as it was quick and painless.

All that took place in my head. When I finally got my voice back, I said, "Okay, Josh. I trust you, regardless of what happens."

"That's the spirit!" He laughed. "I'm really looking forward to this. It's rare that I get to experience something, anything, for the first time."

Joseph just looked down. Then he said to Joshua, "I'll be okay, right?" I could tell he was starting to feel a bit of stress about what was going to happen.

"You're an angel, Joe. What could possibly go wrong?" Joshua said to him matter-of-factly.

"So now what?" I asked. "And where are we going, exactly?"

"You'll see soon enough," he answered. "Okay, guys, are you ready for this?" he asked optimistically.

"No," I said.

"Me neither," Joseph chimed in.

"Good, we're all set then," he said with a laugh. "Everyone hold hands. This could be a bit of a bumpy ride," he said as we clasped hands together.

All of a sudden, a wicked wind started swirling around my apartment, scattering all my carefully prepared questions and overturning the ashtrays. I saw Poppy go flying around the room in a circle near the ceiling. She actually seemed to be enjoying it by the way she was frantically moving her legs and wagging her tail. Was Poppy coming too? No time to think about that. There were ashes everywhere, and the wind (where was it coming from?) started to form into a small tornado-like structure.

I lost consciousness as the small tornado lifted us out of apartment building and into the clouds.

Chapter Fourteen

Ouch. My eyes were closed, but I could tell I was conscious again. I was almost afraid to open my eyes. My last memory was that Joshua was taking me and Joseph back to first-century Palestine so that we could see him as Jesus the Nazarene doing—what? What exactly would we be seeing?

My mind worked lickety-split as I quickly reviewed what I knew about Jesus the Nazarene from so many years ago at Bible college.

I still had my eyes closed and was mentally checking my physical state. I was able to slightly move my arms and legs, which was good, and my mind seemed to be working okay, but I was feeling some unexpected aches and pains throughout my entire body.

I had pretty much convinced myself that I was alive, and I remembered that Joshua had told me and Joseph that we were all going to be "transported" back to the time Jesus the Nazarene (who was actually Joshua—what?) was carrying out his "mission" on earth. That would have put us around AD 30, I figured.

I slowly opened my eyes. I heard the tinkling of a bell just as I started to look around, and there was a big—goat, sticking out its tongue to lick my face. "Yuck," I thought as I ducked the tongue, scrambled to my feet, and looked around for Joshua and Joseph. They were nowhere to be seen. What the . . . ? I felt somewhat uncomfortable, so I looked down and noticed I was no longer wearing my jeans and T-shirt. I noticed instead with amazement that I was wearing a fancy robe with a belt holding it together. I saw that I had on a pair of sandals laced up almost to my knees. I had my right toe amputated years ago when I first discovered I had diabetes, and sure enough, it was still missing. I quickly wondered if anything *else* was missing, so I reached inside my robe and checked on Ranger Bob (the name I had given my thing when I was a teenager). Whew! Still there. *That* was good news. But in doing that checking, I noticed I had on some kind of loincloth—to keep the Ranger from swinging around, I guess.

So I was alive and, from the looks of it, somewhere in the Middle East. I looked across the countryside and saw three or four herds of goats. "Where were all the people?" I wondered. As my eyes started to focus, I began to see more life on the horizon. There were definitely some human forms with the goats, and farther on the horizon, I saw people walking past one another on a road, going in different directions. It was hot and humid. "Must be a hundred degrees, maybe more," I thought.

For the first time since I had struggled up and looked around, I became scared. Scared shitless. What happened? More importantly, where was Joshua? Was I stranded here? And how could I be certain I wasn't just transported to the Middle East in the present time? Like, was it the late AD 20s or 2016? I wasn't sure yet.

Suddenly there was a loud *whooshing* sound, and I turned around to see where it was coming from. Not ten feet away, I saw two human types, both wearing robes and both curled up on the ground. It looked like steam was rising from their bodies. I took a step closer and recognized the toothless visage of Joseph the angel. "Certainly the other guy must be Joshua!" I thought.

The guy curled up next to Joseph, opened his eyes, blinked a few times, and finally focused on me.

"Yeah, it's me," Joshua said.

"Whew," I thought again. "Thank God you're here, Josh," I said. "I was starting to get worried."

He looked over at Joseph's still body and said, "Joe! You okay?"

Joseph stirred, moved from a curled-up position to a sitting one, and said, "Yeah, I think so. What the hell just happened?"

"We did it, Joe," said Joshua. "We're back in the day!"

I was starting to feel a bit left out. "Hello? Remember me?" I asked.

"Yeah, yeah, Rog. We all made it in one piece. I was particularly worried about *you*," he said.

I was in *way* over my head. Was this really happening? It must be. Who was it who said, "I think, therefore I am?" Descartes? "Was Descartes even alive yet?" I wondered. Must not be. I think I was a few centuries off the mark on that one. But still, I was *thinking*, so I must be—alive, I guess. Actually, I was sure of it. I looked over at Joshua and Joseph.

Joseph said, "Well, Lord, what do we do now?"

"Follow me," he said.

So we did.

Chapter Fifteen

We followed Joshua as he headed toward the road in the distance. The closer we got, the more I could see that there were tons of people on the road, going one way or the other. Donkeys pulling carts filled with—grain, I guess. And wooden barrels filled with—I didn't know. Children were walking with their parents and relatives, ragtag dogs barking aimlessly. It was quite the scene.

We got to the road, and Joshua took the lead. He asked one of the travelers where they were headed. "Capernaum," one man said. Capernaum! I immediately thought of something I remembered reading in the Bible about an amazing healing performed by Jesus the Nazarene there.

"That's where we're headed," Joshua said to Joseph and me. So we took our place in the human train and started walking. Within half an hour, we entered the city of Capernaum. The first thing I noticed was the soldiers. Roman soldiers appeared almost everywhere—all looking pretty snazzy in their light armor, helmets, sandals, shin guards ("Did they ever play soccer?" I wondered), and short but deadly looking long daggers attached to their ornate belts. "Pretty cool looking, if you ask me," I thought. Nobody did.

Did Joshua know where we were going?

"Yeah, I know now. I remember," he said. "But we have to be very careful. Keep your hoodie up at all times, and try to keep your face hidden."

"Why me?" I asked.

"Because you're a pale-skinned guy with a weird haircut and a big toe missing. Just try not to stick out," he admonished me.

I looked at Joshua and noticed that his appearance was different from how he appeared in my apartment. Instead of a First Cut haircut, his hair was hanging down beyond the neckline of his robe, and his carefully trimmed goatee was now a full beard. A scraggly beard. "Strange," I thought. "How did *that* happen?" I decided not to pursue it.

We weaved our way through the busy streets. There were all sorts of vendors and small shops, mostly set up near houses and government buildings. It kind of reminded me of a scene from the TV show *Homeland*, when Kerry would walk through the marketplace in Tehran. Chickens and dogs and kids were everywhere. It was quite the sight, for me anyway.

Joshua kept threading his way deftly through the crowd, with Joseph and me struggling to stay up with him. I saw a house up ahead, a pretty big house—it seemed to me—with a throng of people gathered at the front entrance. Something was going on in there, and Joshua was leading us to that house. I looked up and noticed a bunch of people on the garden patio situated on the flat roof. What was everybody doing here?

Silly question. Of course they were here because the almost famous Nazarene was inside. Omigod! Was I really going to see the real Jesus? Wait. I was *with* the real Jesus, wasn't I? I felt as if I was on a movie set. It was getting pretty confusing. I looked more carefully and saw about half a dozen Roman soldiers near the edge of the crowd at the front entrance. "Making sure that things remain peaceful," I thought.

"Yes," said Joshua. "And let's make sure and keep it that way."

We followed Joshua as he wormed his way into the crowd and then through it to the inside of the main room. We weren't making any friends. Joshua paid no attention. He squished in between two people sitting near the front wall of the room and elbowed them enough so as to make two small spaces for Joseph and me. I tried not to be self-conscious, but I couldn't help it. We were being a bit rude, for sure. But Joshua was looking intently at the man in the middle of the room.

"Holy *shit*!" I thought. I knew I was looking at Jesus the Nazarene. And here I was sitting with . . . with who? The Son of God, known on earth as Jesus? That's the best I could do. The room was hushed, and his words started to swirl around me. I could hear him clearly. Some people near the room's walls were standing, but most were sitting down, especially those closest to the Nazarene.

The thing is, of course, I had no idea what he was saying, at least at first.

He was teaching in Aramaic, I figured. I could tell the crowd was listening intently, hanging on every word in a hushed silence. I sneaked a glance at Joshua, and he, too, was listening intently. He had that wry smile on his face. I could only imagine what it must be like to be watching yourself! The very thought made me feel uneasy inside, but he seemed to be enraptured. I glanced at Joseph, and he seemed, well, nonplussed. Did he not understand Aramaic? I figured he must have, but why did he seem so disinterested?

The Nazarene was speaking in a hushed but forceful tone. His words enveloped me. I felt as if I was in a dream state. After about forty-five minutes of listening to him, I almost fell into a trance. My mind was quiet, and I started to drift off. It wasn't that I was bored—well, maybe a little bit—but I felt fatigued from the "trip," and I was getting a bit light-headed.

I jerked awake. The Nazarene was finished talking, as far as I could tell, and one guy from the crowd was quietly asking him a question. I was tempted to whisper and ask Joshua what was being asked and how the Nazarene was responding, but I thought better of it. I'm sure he would fill me in when we got back to the apartment—*if* we ever got back to the apartment. I was starting to get uneasy about that possibility.

Joshua moved suddenly, trying to get in a more comfortable position. The crowd was hushed, and the Nazarene continued to speak. As Joshua moved, he let out an almost inaudible *fffrrrrttt*! I was so embarrassed for him, and I felt terribly self-conscious. But I quickly recovered, glanced over at him, and well, I couldn't help it. "The spider bit the frog," I quipped, trying hard not to break into uncontrollable laughter.

A few heads in the crowd moved to see who it was.

I was looking at Joshua as his shoulders started to shake. "Oh no!" I thought. "He's going to break into a loud laughing spell!" I was scared. What would happen if the Nazarene were to see Joshua? All sorts of bad things started crowding themselves into my mind, most along the lines of *Bill and Ted's Excellent Adventure* or *Hot Tub Time Machine*. "This could get dangerous," I thought.

Jesus the Nazarene noticed the murmuring of the crowd. He stopped speaking, looked right at Joshua, who was still trying hard not to break into audible laughter, and winked. My mind could barely comprehend what had just happened. Joshua, the Son of God, was sitting in that house listening to—himself? I couldn't grasp the Big Picture. Jesus the Nazarene had winked at Joshua, who used to be—Jesus the Nazarene!

I was relieved when Jesus went back to his quiet teaching as Joshua regained control. Joshua looked at me and whispered, "Spider bit the frog? Really, Rog?" He started to stifle a laugh again and quickly regained his composure. I was pretty sure he wasn't going to let me forget this scene.

Suddenly a good-sized chunk of clay dropped from the ceiling, narrowly missing one of the small children gathered around the feet of Jesus. The child scampered away as another fist-sized chunk dropped and crashed to the hard floor. What the . . . ? I glanced up with the rest of the crowd and saw a small hole developing in the ceiling. People started scrambling to get away from the middle of the room as more and more chunks of hardened clay hit the floor. Now there was a *huge* hole opening up in the ceiling. An earthquake, maybe?

Then I saw a human head peeking from the hole in the ceiling into the room below. The Nazarene, too, was looking up. He had the same wry smile on his face that Joshua had a moment ago. They really were like twin brothers. "What am I thinking?" I thought. *"They were the same person!"* But now there were two of them. My mind couldn't wrap itself around that. And it wasn't wrapping itself much better around what was happening. The hole was now quite large in the ceiling, and I saw three heads peering down through it.

It was then that I caught on to what was happening. I had read about this incident before when Jesus the Nazarene was teaching in a house in Capernaum. As I watched in astonishment, a big hole developed in the roof. Then four young men started lowering a guy into the middle of the house's main room using a mat tied to ropes. The man was paralyzed. "Yes!" I thought. "This is when Jesus heals the quadriplegic!" I watched in amazement and wonder as the man was carefully lowered down in front of the Nazarene. I knew what was going to happen, I figured, but I was in a trance, watching it actually take place right in front of me.

The paralyzed guy was now resting on the floor. One of the guys shouted down from the roof. He told Jesus that this was his brother and that he had been paralyzed in a swimming accident years earlier. He couldn't get his brother close enough to Jesus because of the crowd, so he decided to ask some friends to help him bring his brother to the house and smash a hole in the roof so that Jesus might heal him.

The Nazarene knelt down beside the man. From my vantage point, it appeared that he had tears in his eyes. They *both* had tears in their eyes. I looked over at Joshua and saw that *he, too,* had tears in his eyes. Then I noticed that *I* had tears in my eyes! Joseph, too, raised his hand to his eyes as if trying to hide that he was pretty emotional too.

Jesus was saying something softly to the man on the floor. Within a minute, the paralyzed man started to move one of his legs and then the other one. I'd never seen someone actually get healed before.

Jesus the Nazarene continued talking quietly to the man as the rest of his body stirred to life. After about a minute, he helped the man to his feet, fully able to move on his own. I was stunned! The crowd went wild!

The man was tentatively trying to walk a few steps when all hell broke loose. The Roman soldiers outside the front entrance of the house had heard the uproar and must have figured that something seditious was happening inside. Joshua got up quickly, followed by Joseph and then me. We crunched our way into the crowd, all headed for the front entrance as one bewildered herd. As we got to the front steps, two Roman soldiers were furiously looking for anyone who might look suspicious. That would be everyone. But for some reason, they focused on me, Joshua, and Joseph.

Omigod! We were about to be arrested! What would happen *then*? Was I going to be stuck in first-century Palestine for the rest of my life? In jail? I swung around to look at Joshua. His eyes were wide, and his mouth was open, as if surprised. He looked at me with a wild look in his eyes. I started to think that everything was going to be okay because—well, because he was the Son of God and could certainly get us out of this mess. I looked at him as if to ask, "What do we do now?" He hesitated for a second as the Roman soldiers kept coming right at us, shoving the crowd aside and with their sharp sword knives in hand.

As I was looking at him quizzically, waiting for him to do something, he looked me straight in the eye and said, in a loud whisper, "Run!"

What the *hell*? *Run*? I looked at him with astonishment and fear. Why? Were we in trouble?

He scrambled over to my side and whispered in my ear, "Not *us*," he said. "*You*! Now *run*!"

"What about *them*?" I thought quickly.

Suddenly I heard a *poof* sound, followed quickly by another *poof*. I had just forced my legs to start moving. I looked back at Joshua and Joseph and—they weren't there!

"Holy *shit*!" I thought as I tried to force my way through the crowd away from the oncoming Roman soldiers, who were now screaming for the crowd to clear so that they could apprehend me. I was stupefied. My mind shut down, and I just kept clawing my way through the crowd. I was literally scared shitless.

I broke through the crowd and started running in the narrow street. I took a quick left, then a right, and hastened a look back. The Roman soldiers were gaining on me, not more than ten yards away. They, too, had broken through the crowd and were now just seconds from throwing me to the ground. I turned away from the soldiers and tried to keep going when a hand grabbed the scruff of my robe and pulled me hard.

My last thought before I passed out was, "I'm *screwed*."

Chapter Sixteen

I came to and found myself lying on the ground in a small dark room. "*Shhhhh!*" a voice commanded me. Was I being arrested? Was I about to be stabbed in the eye by one of those short, sharp, pointy swords?

It was dark and quiet in the room. I heard quite the commotion outside in the streets, but it was calm inside. What was happening? Where was Joshua? Joshua was my lifeline. Was I about to die? I wondered.

I lay there for a good ten minutes, conscious of a man with a strong right hand holding my face to the ground as he knelt beside me. After ten minutes or so, he loosened his hold on my neck. My eyes were growing accustomed to the dark, and I noticed the form of man, now standing and peeking out through the almost-closed door. He stayed at the door for another five minutes before coming back to me. I was sitting up now, my robe was all dirty, and I was sweating that fear sweat. I could still hear the muffled sound of people running and talking excitedly outside in the street. I kept quiet. Finally the guy motioned for me to follow him in.

Chapter Seventeen

Whoever this guy was, I figured he must have saved my life. We were in a dark room of a house, it looked like, and he pushed me forward toward the stairs leading to an upper room. He knocked on the door of the upper room three times in quick succession and then whispered something through the door. After a second, the door opened a crack, and then it opened fully. He pushed me gently inside, came in himself, and closed the door. There was a big plank of wood that one of the guys in the room placed firmly in its allotted slot. No one was going to get into the room except by repeated hammering with a battering ram.

I ventured a glance around the room and saw about eight men and one woman. A woman? I let that thought pass and studied the faces of a couple of the men. Wait! I glanced back at the woman. I couldn't help it. She was stunning! Late teens, I guessed, and she must have been one of the most beautiful women I had ever laid eyes on.

The man who had saved my skin put his hand on my shoulder from behind, breaking my gaze.

"Who *are* you?" he asked abruptly.

Wait! What the hell was happening? I understood everything that was being said to me! How could that be?

Listening to myself think this, I realized that I wasn't speaking English. Like, I was *thinking* in English, but my guess was that I was speaking and understanding in Aramaic. I was pretty sure that something magical was happening. I would form a sentence in English in my mind, but when it came out my mouth, it was in Aramaic.

I tried to move my mouth, but nothing came out.

A few of the men said in unison, "Who *are* you?"

One stepped forward and said, "Who are you, and what are you doing here?"

Words started to form in my mouth. "Where am I?" I asked.

"Never mind that," the guy behind me said. He came around to stand in front of me and looked intently at my face. "Who are you, and what are you doing here?"

I didn't know how to answer that. I was here because someone dragged me from the street and brought me here. I said, "I'm not sure what's happening. Who *are* you guys?" I asked, glancing over at the woman.

The man who had dragged me into the house spoke up.

"My name is Peter. We are all followers of Jesus the Nazarene."

Now I was starting to catch on. Did Joshua somehow arrange for this to happen? I hoped I would have the opportunity to ask him some day. Some day? My heart sank.

"My name is . . . Rog," I said tentatively.

"Rahj," I heard a couple of them murmur. "Are you a Jew?"

Hmmm . . . I knew I had Jewish roots somewhere down my family line, but I didn't think I was really a Jew.

"No," I answered. "I come from . . ."

What was I going to say? That I was a time traveler from the future? I was pretty sure that wasn't going to fly.

"I'm just visiting Capernaum from . . . Jerusalem," I said, a bit proud of myself for my recovery.

"Jerusalem?" Peter said. "Welcome, then."

"What's happening here?" I asked.

"We are followers of Jesus the Nazarene," Peter repeated. "He's being followed everywhere he goes by Roman soldiers, who fear that he may be fomenting rebellion."

"Rebellion?" I thought. Yeah, that made sense. It's like, that really was the reason that Joshua (or Jesus) was put to death.

Peter seemed to be the spokesman for the group. I sneaked another glance over at the woman and then looked back at Peter.

"So are you guys what they call apostles?"

No response.

I tried again. "So are you the ones whom Jesus the Nazarene called to leave everything and follow him?"

This time Peter responded. "Yes," he said. "How do you know that?" He sounded suspicious.

"Just an educated guess," I said. "So what happens now?" I was anxious to figure out what was going on so I could think of some way to get home.

"We wait for our Master," Peter said.

Chapter Eighteen

We sat in virtual silence for at least an hour. The men were whispering among themselves, but I couldn't hear what they were saying. The tension in the room was palpable, and I could tell that they didn't seem all that comfortable with me there either.

Suddenly, there were three quick knocks on the upper-room door. "Roman soldiers?" I thought wildly.

Peter got up from where he was sitting and asked through the door, "Who's there?"

"It's me," a voice answered.

Without hesitation Peter opened the door, and in walked—Joshua! I was ecstatic! Finally, we could go home!

Peter embraced Jesus the Nazarene and said, "Yeshua. Thank God you made it back here in one piece."

Jesus of Nazareth stepped into the room, going around and hugging his closest followers. When he got to the woman, he stopped and gave her a lingering embrace. He kissed her *(on the lips!)*, and I barely made out his whisper. "Miriam," he said, "I'm so glad you made it here safely."

Miriam? Could that be Mary Magdalene? It *had* to be! No wonder he was head over heels in love with this woman. She was so . . .

He stopped and looked at me intently. "Who's this?" he asked.

Oh no! He didn't know who I was! Now what?

Reading my mind and feeling my desperation, he whispered to me in English, "It's okay, Rog. I think I know what's going on here."

"Thank God!" I thought. But this was still quite the confusing mess.

"Where's Joshua?" he asked. "Or if it makes you feel any better, where am *I*?"

This conversation was starting to take on an *Alice in Wonderland* feel to it. Who was who, and who was—I could make some sense out of it, but I'm sure his followers were baffled.

He continued, "Not to worry, Rog. I'll make sure you get back home again."

Get back home again? I didn't know what to think. Here I was talking to Jesus when I was still in the middle of an interview with—Jesus (Joshua, that is) over two thousand years from now! This was too much for a human mind to handle—at least *my* human mind.

Jesus turned to his followers and said, "I'm taking Rahj here up to one of our secret places. We need to be alone. Are you guys okay with waiting here for me to get back?"

"Yes," Peter answered for the group. I got the feeling that he was a little down after hearing that Jesus was taking off again. I guess in their world there was a lot of waiting around.

He turned to me and asked, "Ready, Rog?" I nodded. "Then follow me."

Chapter Nineteen

We both had our robe hoodies pulled over our heads as we ventured into the streets. We made our way through the throng and headed out of town.

The crowd had thinned considerably, and I was able to relax a bit. We hadn't spoken since we left the upper room. But now I felt compelled.

"So do you know what's going on?" I ventured.

"No," he said. I kept walking, but he glanced at me and said, "I know it must be very confusing to you right now, Rog, but it's me."

It's me? I was . . . very confused.

We walked along in silence.

Within forty-five minutes or so, he stopped. "Over there," he said.

I looked and saw a small worn path leading into the bush. We took the path and walked for a while before we came to a small cove, an open spot surrounded by small trees and bushes. No one was there, and no one could see us from the faraway road. Was this the secret place he had talked about with his followers?

"Yes," he said. "It is. I didn't mean to lead you astray earlier, but I must admit I'm not sure what is really happening. Can you fill me in?"

I began to tell him about Joseph the angel and how I had been chosen to interview Jesus in the twenty-first century. I told him that he had come back to earth so that he could "set the record straight" and try to clear up all the crap that had been going on in his name for centuries.

His eyes widened as I told him the details about how I ended up in first-century Palestine. He stayed quiet for a minute after I finished telling him what was happening. He looked at me and said, "That Dad of mine! Actually, I'm not surprised at all at what he's up to. He's so creative, and while I don't exactly know right now what happens to my message, I'm not at all surprised to hear that things start breaking bad soon after I finish up here. After all, I've learned that whenever human beings get involved in something, especially men, they tend to screw it up."

"Hey," I thought, "that's what Joshua said!"

"No surprise there either, is there? I mean, Joshua is me after all," he said.

Joshua is me. What a concept. I tried not to think about it too deeply.

I looked at Jesus and said, "I just want to go home, please. I'm scared."

"Don't be afraid," he said. "I'll make sure you get back home. Take both of my hands."

I did. Suddenly, a wild wind started blowing violently just like it did in my apartment so many hours ago. I held onto his hands for dear life, my feet leaving the caked soil and my legs going horizontal to the ground. I felt my robe fly open as the wind ripped through my hair.

Just as I was about to lose consciousness, he let go of my hand. I went flying off into space, mouth agape and eyes watering so much that I couldn't see anything. I closed my eyes and waited for whatever was in store for me.

Chapter Twenty

fter what seemed like just a few seconds, I landed with a *thump* somewhere. Hard. "Now what?" I thought.

I kept my eyes closed and went through the whole physical inventory thing. I moved my legs a bit. They were working—then my arms and fingers. I opened my eyes and quickly looked down to where my left big toe should be. It had to be amputated a few years ago when my diabetes was out of control. It was still gone. Bummer. But then I took a quick glance around at my surroundings. I was on a balcony of some sort.

Wait a minute. It was *my* balcony. I was home!

As soon as I got to my knees and then my feet, the balcony door opened. There was Joshua, quickly followed by Joseph.

"Rog! Are you okay?" Joshua asked excitedly.

I pushed by them and walked through the balcony door into the living room.

"Yeah, I think so," I muttered. Then I said, "But one thing bothers me. Now we've lost, what? Eight hours?" I calculated quickly.

Joshua chuckled and said, "Actually, Rog, we've only been gone thirteen minutes."

What? Really? I walked into the kitchen area and looked at the clock hanging on the wall. It was 12:30 p.m. Holy shit! He was right. What seemed like hours had turned out to be only minutes.

"That's how it works, Rog," he said.

I was starting to gain my bearings a bit. I tried to wrap my brain around the fact that we had actually gone back in time almost two thousand years.

Joshua knew what I was thinking and let me revel in it for a minute. Then he said, "It *was* pretty exciting, don't you think?"

I had to admit things had worked out pretty well, all things considered. I had to be careful in answering his question, though.

I wondered about what had happened with Jesus. I thought to myself, "Who was it, really, who helped me?"

I tried to answer my own question.

"I guess it was Jes . . . ," I started but abruptly stopped. "I mean, *you* helped me. But who is *you*?" I asked ungrammatically. I didn't know how else to say it.

Joshua looked at me and said, "Let's sit back down at the kitchen table, and I'll tell you all about it."

Chapter Twenty-One

First I needed a beer. Joshua wanted one too. So did Joe. I went to the fridge and grabbed three beers. Where was the hard stuff when you needed it? I had decided a few years ago to stick to beer and wine. Bourbon had been my downfall. I ended up doing things that I don't even remember doing—or saying. It was too embarrassing—and dangerous, I figured.

Still, I wished I could have two or three quick shots right now. "But, just as well," I thought. I wanted to stay sharp for the rest of our time together.

We sat back down at the kitchen table.

"I saw Mary Magdalene," I said. It was the first thing that popped into my mind.

"She was very, very special to me," Joshua said. "I can hardly wait to see her again. I couldn't even bear to see her when we went back. It just would have been too much for me to handle."

"The healing I saw you perform was amazing!" I said, changing the subject.

"I wanted you both to see that," Joshua said as he glanced over at Joseph.

Joseph had been sitting there quietly. My heart went out to him. My thoughts went back to the psych ward where we had met. I remember hearing some of the other inmates making fun of him because of his looks, especially the fact that he had no teeth. One time, after overhearing three guys laughing and joking about him by name, I went up to them and gave them shit. "Why are you making fun of Joseph?" I asked. "Try and put yourself in his shoes for a moment. If you can't say anything nice about him, then just shut the hell up."

They slinked away.

Joseph reached for my pack of cigarettes and lit three up. He passed one to me and one to Joshua. I wondered if he knew what I was remembering because he had a sad look on his face. He took a drag and exhaled a rich blue stream of smoke. Then he looked over at me and smiled. My heart melted. I unexpectedly heard my mind saying a prayer for him. I even surprised myself.

I settled my thoughts down and said to Joshua, "When I think back now about being in the past with you, I understand so much better. Seeing you, well, Jesus, perform that healing and then getting me home was just . . ." I couldn't put it into words.

So I tried again.

"I have this sense now that the interview is going to go really well," I said. "Now that I've actually been there and seen you in action, that makes a world of difference. Now I think I can really relate to some of the things you're telling me."

Chapter Twenty-Two

I thought about what I had just experienced and decided to ask a question not in my notes.

"I'd like to hear you talk about the healings you performed like the one I just witnessed. What was your motivation for healing people?"

Joshua lowered his eyes to the table and then raised his head and said, "The healings I did were meant to underscore the importance of the Kingdom of God message: *Don't be afraid or anxious about anything in this life, including your own death. Life continues.* But how can you live your life with that hope if you're chronically sick, or in pain, or suffering, or have serious mental health issues? I was deeply moved by people with illnesses, both physical and mental; I saw so much despair and lack of hope in so many people who came to me. But I learned that I could literally change their lives by healing them. I believe that when people were healed, such healings validated the message that God chose me to proclaim. And, to be fair, when I use the word 'heal,' I'm really referring to a very common phenomenon. People can heal themselves if they believe they *can* be healed. So much of healing is really just having faith that one really *can* be healed."

"Just having faith can actually heal you?"

"It sure helps. It's amazing to see how the body is designed to heal itself, and having faith in that reality can enhance a person's chance of being healed. Often times I told people, 'Your faith has made you whole.' There is a direct correlation between one's state of mind and one's physical health. I was very curious about human thinking and behavior back then, being human myself. At times I was puzzled by people's responses when I would heal them. Many times I told the people I healed that it was *their faith* that made them whole. I learned a lot about human nature and about myself when I would heal someone. One time an older woman tried to squeeze through the crowd to touch me. She had—well, I guess you could say she had—a woman-specific problem, and it was literally killing her. I could almost hear her saying to herself, 'If I could just touch the hem of his blue jeans, I bet I would be healed.'"

"You wore blue jeans?"

"No, I wore one of those stupid robes like everyone else wore at the time. I wasn't that impressed with what passed for 'fashion' in those days. I'm just trying to liven up the story a bit for you."

"So what happened next?" I asked.

"Well, she tried her best to get close enough to me to touch my robe as I passed by, and eventually she did."

"Don't you hate it when people sneak into the line at the movie theater or bully their way to the front of the stage at a concert?"

"Yeah," he responded. "I hate it when that happens. I always had all sorts of people trying to touch me. Usually I didn't notice it all that much, but when that woman touched the tassels on my robe, I actually felt drained of energy. So, curious about who needed all that energy to be healed, I turned around and asked the crowd, 'Who touched my robe?'

"About a dozen people raised their hands and said, 'I did! I did! No, it was *me*! No way, José, it was *me*!'

"I said to the crowd, 'What the . . . ? Just tell me who touched me *last*, okay?'

"After a few more 'I dids,' this woman looked up at me and said, 'I guess that would be me.' She slowly got up with a magnificent smile on her face and said, 'Thanks for healing me. I just figured I would be healed if I could touch your robe.' I was a bit puzzled by how much energy she drained off me, but I always leave that kind of stuff to my Dad. Believe me, he has it all figured out."

I remembered something about that incident and what some Christians had to say about it.

"I've heard a few Christians say over the years that you really knew who it was who touched you, but you were just pretending not to know so that you could use her as an object lesson for faith."

"Yeah, I've heard that too, mostly from those Christians who believe that I was God. But God didn't choose me to merely come and heal people. God chose me to proclaim the Kingdom of God and to *show* people how much he cares about every individual human being. By healing people I was able to show by what I *did* that God's love is unconditional and that his Kingdom is available here on earth. *The Kingdom of God is not about life after death; it's about living life to the fullest right now.*"

I started to ask another question, but Poppy was silently begging me to take her out again. So I told Josh I would be back in a jiff, and we headed out.

Chapter Twenty-Three

I asked, "Okay, Josh, can we talk about something that's very controversial?"

Joshua knew exactly what I wanted to ask him about.

"I didn't come to start a religion. In fact, I spent a great deal of time railing *against* religion, especially the religious leaders and priests—at their hypocrisy and how they delighted in keeping their followers under a yoke of laws, rules, and guilt."

He looked down at the table and then back at me.

"Since the beginning of time, human beings have tried to come up with the answers to the basic questions we all face: Why are we here? What happens after we die? What is God like? *Is* there a God? All religions have specific rules, rituals, and doctrines to follow, designed to help secure your place in what you guys call 'heaven.' But no religion has a corner on the truth. Every religion is man-made and made for men."

Joshua looked over at Joseph and then back at me.

"Religions throughout history, including Christianity, have been guilty of promoting hatred, war, violence, ignorance, and intolerance more than any other force, movement, or ideology I can think of. In essence, religion is man's attempt to find God—to fill the vacuum that exists in each human heart, which can only be filled by God's spirit. The problem is, well, a *human* one. Religion attempts to make contact with God through rituals, creeds, dogmas, pomp, and ceremony. And it has failed miserably."

"And, of course, they're the big hats," I quipped.

"Yeah, the big hats, the robes, the cathedrals—it would just be sadly hilarious except for the damage it's done to people down through the ages. It becomes all about power and control. It pisses me off just to be talking about it. Can you imagine how God has felt about religion throughout human history?"

No, I couldn't. So many thoughts were going through my head. I guess he wasn't focusing on my thoughts, because he just kept going.

"What God is hoping, what his Dream is, is that people will develop a personal *awareness* of him without the structure of religion—no middle men, no priests, no one absolving you of your sins. Just like in any relationship, it's just you and God. *That's* what I came to tell people. You can have a personal awareness of God without all the trappings of 'religion.' God's Dream is that religions will eventually die out. Religion is a *barrier* to seeking God, not a bridge."

Okay, now he was blowing my mind. The end of religion? I couldn't begin to imagine what that would even look like.

"Look, Rog, when it comes to the God of the Bible, or of any religion, I am an atheist."

My jaw dropped. "An atheist? *For chrissake*, Josh, what are you talking about?" Here I was interviewing Jesus Christ, and he just told me he's an atheist!

"No one believes in Zeus or Thor or Hercules anymore. Everyone is an atheist when it comes to those gods. I'm just saying that I am an atheist when it comes to the god of any religion, including the god of the Bible. Those gods have nothing to do with *who God really is*. My point is that having an awareness of God has nothing to do with the classical sense of a 'religion.' All religions ever invented by men have been used as a form of control over others since the beginning of time: power, authority, prestige, and of course, money—lots and lots of money."

"Okay, man, I think I'm starting to get it. So you're saying that you agree with John Lennon when he encouraged us to imagine a world without religion?"

"Yeah, I do. The thing is, when one man or group of men starts to take over and vaunt themselves up as the 'leaders' of a group of followers, that's when things begin to go sideways. Power over others changes people—and never for the better."

Joshua got up from his chair and took a few steps into the living room. This time he lied down on the couch with one hand over his eyes. Is he really tired?

"No, just thinking," he said.

"Are you bummed out about talking about religion?"

"Yeah, I guess I am—not so much bummed out, but it just makes me sad to think about all the terrible things that have been done in my name over the centuries and how it reflects so poorly on God."

"I've heard many people say over the years that being religious or part of a religion is benign—that it doesn't hurt anyone, so what's the big deal?"

"You know the score with that, Rog. Bad things seem to go hand in hand with religion: wars, hatred, ethnic cleansing, suicide bombers, intolerance, and killing. Take 9/11, for example. Those guys who crashed those planes into the World Trade Center towers were the epitome of what happens with religion. They truly believed that they were being obedient to God. What they did was grounded in what they believed. I can't think of a strong enough word to use when I think about those kinds of atrocities."

I kept my mouth shut. He seemed pretty upset.

"Do you think that a suicide bomber thinks he's evil or even that he's *doing* something evil? Or that he's committing an atrocity? Of course not; he believes that he's serving God or Allah or whomever."

I thought I'd try and lighten the mood a bit. He was agitated.

"Someone once told me that God's name is Harold."

Joshua got up from the couch, stood up, and came back to the kitchen table.

"Harold? I don't get it."

"Yeah, from the prayer you taught your followers to pray, 'Our Father, who art in heaven, Harold be thy name.'"

Joshua threw his head back and laughed. "Yeah, okay, Rog, thanks for that.

"Look, religion is a double-edged sword. It's a virtue that people want to find God and meaning in their lives, but when any kind of hierarchy or organization starts to take place, watch out. Religion has done tremendous harm and perpetuated the worse kind of torment on people. It leads people to think that they are doing 'God's Work,' however they define that."

"But . . . but, like, what about all the *good* things that Christianity has done for people over the centuries: building hospitals and helping the poor—that kind of thing. Doesn't that suggest that Christianity is a force for good in the world?"

"No. The Christian religion has at times been a force for good in the lives of people over the years. *But at what cost?* The 'good' that has been done does not somehow mysteriously cancel out the disgust Christians had, and continue to have, toward those who are not Christians or the *right kind* of Christians. Consider the witch burnings, the torture and murder of 'heretics,' throughout the centuries, the subjugation of women, and the killing of homosexuals. The list is endless. Christianity has destroyed countless lives more than it has 'helped' humanity."

Okay, so Joshua was pulling no punches in trashing organized religion, including Christianity. But he's Jesus Christ, *for chrissake*! Who's going to pay any attention at all to him if he keeps this up?

"Okay, Josh, I'm with you on this, and I pretty much totally agree with what you're saying. But what can you possibly *do* about it?" I didn't get that part.

I saw Joshua's shoulders go slack as if he was trying to gain control of his emotions. He placed his hands on the kitchen table and took a deep breath, holding it in for a few seconds before exhaling.

"I hear you, Rog. My hope is that what's happening here today will be the beginning of a new dialogue among Christians and those of other religions—a dialogue designed to lead people to question their religious convictions. Religions will continue to exist as long as human beings exist until people start growing up and seeing that religion is both delusional and dangerous. The Christian religion is based on guilt, fear, power, control, and money. The Kingdom of God message I proclaimed is the antithesis of contemporary Christianity. God's Dream is that religion will eventually cease to exist."

Chapter Twenty-Four

I asked, "Okay, Josh, if we're to take you seriously about living our lives to the fullest and without anxiety or fear, where would one even begin?"

"Good question, Rog. Here's what I would recommend: Start with the Sermon on the Mount in Matthew's Gospel in the Bible. There was no one-time event where I gave a teaching on all that's in there, but it's a collection of teachings that did come from me. Some parts of it were made up or added by the Gospel writers and scribes decades after I died—like the teaching about divorce, which is just so much male-chauvinistic crap. Use your common sense and read a few books about it. You'll figure it out."

"Okay, so we should focus on the Sermon on the Mount. Then what?"

"If people could just learn to live their lives by what I taught in that collection of teachings, it would go a long way to helping you learn how to live life to the fullest and really enjoy life each day—to live out the values of the Kingdom of God. It's not rocket science, Rog. Most of what I taught is clear to any reasonable person. The hard part is to *live* it."

"Okay, so can you remind me and anyone who might read this what you said in that sermon?"

"Sure. I'll give it to you in a nutshell."

Joshua lowered his head for a moment and then stood up and began walking around the living room.

"Blessed are the poor, for theirs is the Kingdom of—"

"Whoa, whoa, hold on, dude! You lost me already! What the heck does the word 'Blessed' even mean? Like, can't you just tell me what you taught in that sermon in plain English?"

Joshua stopped in his tracks and looked at me askew.

"Well, yeah, I guess so. How about this: Be happy if you're poor—"

"C'mon, Josh, what gives? Be happy if you're poor? What the hell? Just say it as if you actually mean it!"

I was upset, and Joshua knew it. But I was right.

"Geez, Rog, don't have a cow."

"Sorry, man, I just want to hear you say it in a way that I and others will be able to understand."

"Okay, you're right."

He sat back down at the kitchen table and looked me right in the eye. He paused for a moment and then started up again.

"Life here on earth should be a really cool experience. But, you know, for some it is, but for most it's a real struggle. So here's what I meant when I started that teaching: Don't give up when you're at the end of your rope. When you're down and out, ask God for help. Look carefully inside your heart for what God is doing in your life and how much he loves you and cares for you. He'll take care of you.

"When you feel like all is lost, that's when God will pour out his love and compassion on you in a special way, and you'll know intuitively that everything is going to be okay.

"*Always* stand up against injustice wherever you see it. Be it small or large, *do something*! Injustice occurs when people are not treated with dignity and respect. You have to learn to step in and defend the defenseless, speak up when someone is being bullied, encourage the downhearted, give of your time and resources generously. By thinking of and helping other people, you will find God's peace in your life, and you'll be empowering others as well as yourself.

"Always take the high road in your dealings with others. By helping others achieve their goals in life, you help yourself to achieve your own goals.

"Don't be afraid of anything in this life. Trust God to take away all your fear and anxiety. He loves you and is always there for you, even when you're not aware of it, even for those who don't believe he even exists.

"People who are aware of God in their lives are the light of the world. Let your light shine brightly every day by being kind, generous, caring, and compassionate toward others. Be compassionate toward others as God is compassionate toward you.

"You've heard it said, 'Light overcomes darkness.' That is true. As much as possible, be positive about your life and shine on others; have a positive, expectant attitude, even when things aren't going your way.

"Why stockpile money in this life? You can't take any of it with you when you die. Instead, focus on using your money to help others. There's nothing wrong with being comfortable. How about this: only keep enough money to keep yourself comfortable and then give generously to those who are in need, starting with your family and friends. It goes back to treating others the way you want to be treated. You can't serve two masters. You have to choose whether you put your trust in God or in money.

"Your eyes are the windows into your soul. If you open up your eyes to this world of wonder, your whole body will be full of light. What I'm telling you is to look deep within yourself for what is true. The Kingdom of God is *within* you. Learn to share in God's Dream and encourage others to as well.

"Accept yourself for who you are. Don't get all caught up in what people wear or how they look. Accept yourself for who you are and accept others for who they are.

"Perhaps most important of all: Don't judge other people. Nobody's perfect. Forgive others when they do you wrong. Try not to be an idiot; don't judge other people, ever.

"Put your entire attention on what God is doing in your life *right now.* Don't worry about what may or may not happen in the future. God will help you through the tough times when those times come.

"To sum it all up: Be aware of God to the best of your ability and as you understand him. And, equally important, treat other people in your life as you want to be treated." Joshua looked over at me with a smile and said, "So, what do you think?"

"Man, Josh, you pulled it together. I know you just kind of summed it up, but I get what you mean when you say you can't go wrong by following what you taught in the Sermon on the Mount. I think that's exactly what I'm going to do after you leave: try to follow your teaching every day."

"Good. That's what I'm hoping, Rog, with this interview. I hope to inspire Christians to take my life and teachings seriously."

I'd never paid all that much attention to the Sermon on the Mount, so his summary of it really hit home. That was partly due to how he just said it plainly in clear English. He gave up on stuff like "Blessed are the meek" or anything with words we never use anymore. It made sense.

Chapter Twenty-Five

But something was missing from what Joshua was telling me. I didn't know exactly how to phrase it, but what I said was, "One thing bothers me, Josh, about what you just told me. Why did you leave out some of the best-known parts of it? Like, almost everyone has heard that you said, 'If someone strikes you on the right cheek, turn to him the other also,' and 'If someone asks you to walk a mile with him, walk with him two miles.' And, of course, your teaching about 'Love your enemies.' Why did you leave those out? Did you teach those things or not?"

Joshua was looking at me with what I took to be admiration.

"I did. The truth is that some of my teachings were directed only to the people I was addressing: first-century Palestinian Jewish peasants. Not everything I taught was meant for all people throughout the ages. The reality is that if one were to take some of my teachings literally today, the results would be disastrous. 'Love your enemies' is a good example. What does that even mean? If you were to follow that teaching today, that you should show kindness for someone out to do you or someone else harm, you could wind up seriously—well, *dead*."

"So why did you teach that in the first place?" I asked.

"To be honest, sometimes I went off the rails and said things just to shake up conventional thinking. I wanted people to reflect on their lives and see how they could truly learn to live their lives to the fullest each day. I kind of regretted saying 'Love your enemies' as soon as it came out of my mouth, but at least it made people think. And here we are two thousand years later still talking about it."

"So it's a good thing that you misspoke because we're still talking about it today?"

"Yeah, kind of. I mean, really, Rog, it doesn't make much sense to love your enemies. It really is impossible to love a person whose hatred or meanness has earned your enmity, or who are just terrible, even evil, people. My point in saying that was to get people to reflect on how God loves human beings without any conditions.

"What I'm saying is that some of the things I taught really make no sense in the twenty-first century. But that doesn't mean those teachings didn't mean something to the original hearers of those teachings. I'll give you an example from one of the teachings you brought up. Take the saying 'If someone asks you to walk a mile with him, walk with him two miles.' What could that possibly mean in today's world? It's hard to say. But for the original hearers, they understood exactly what I meant. Roman political and military rule weighed heavily on the Jewish mind. Jews were, and are, a proud people who believe that they are God's 'chosen people.' A Roman soldier carrying a heavy load could order a Jew standing nearby to carry his stuff for a mile, but no more than a mile, according to Roman law. So the hearers understood that, in order to demonstrate God's love and compassion, they should *volunteer* to carry the soldier's load for another mile. It was a way of standing up to the Roman soldiers, a dignified act of nonviolent resistance to Roman rule. My original listeners understood that.

"The same goes for the teaching 'If someone strikes you on the cheek, turn the other cheek to be struck as well.' Under Roman rule a soldier could strike any Jew for just looking at him sideways. But he could only strike him once under the law. I taught them that they could humiliate any soldier who struck them by turning your head and inviting him to strike you again. It was a subtle but satisfying way to show nonviolent resistance. My hearers understood that. But would that work in today's world? No, of course not. So you see what I mean, Rog? Some of my teachings were not meant to be taken as universal but were directed solely at first-century Palestinian Jews under Roman rule.

"One more thing. The word I used that usually gets translated as 'love' in English actually conveyed the meaning of 'really like' in Aramaic, the language I spoke. The *L* word is *way* too overused today. You can love everything from a sunset to a car to a pet to a person. It almost loses its meaning of 'really liking' something or someone, know what I mean?"

"I do, Josh. I'm glad you're telling me this stuff. I really like you."

"I like you, too, Rog. Ready to move on?"

Chapter Twenty-Six

The interview had started to take on a surreal quality. The things that Jesus Christ was telling me, and now telling the whole twenty-first-century world, were astonishing. I went back to my list of questions.

"As far as your life goes, can you talk about your early years? I really want to hear you talk about what it was like growing up. The way I see it, genes and upbringing are the two greatest factors in how a person turns out in life, and nobody has any say in either one of them."

"You're right; genes and upbringing, along with where you're born and when you're born, are beyond our control. I didn't know much at all about who I was when I was one year old, two years old, or even five years old. I was a regular kid being brought up in a Jewish home by Jewish parents. By the time I was ten or eleven, I did begin to think some crazy thoughts, or thoughts that made me *think* I was crazy. Even at that young age, I believed in God. I mean, I was brought up as a good Jewish boy, right? And my mom, well, don't get me started—"

"Your mom was a bit overbearing, I take it?" I said.

"Yeah, you could say that. I still battle with some guilt feelings when I think about her."

"Really? You feel *guilty*? Can you give an example?"

"No."

"Okay, then," I thought. "Moving right along—"

"I was fortunate to have had an uncle who knew how to read. He was a Pharisee, and not only did he know how to read but he also *loved* reading and then discussing what he read with other Jews in the temple. He taught *me* to read. I began to feel God's *presence* in my life. I didn't know who he was when I was a child, nor did I know who *I* was, but gradually it began to dawn on me that God was somehow personal. That's when I began to pay more attention to things. I did have a sense that I was here on earth for a special purpose. I kept reading over the years and spending time listening to what the religious leaders would be discussing in the synagogue. Then by the time I was fourteen, I was at the synagogue every free moment I had, and I even began to ask questions and enter the discussions with them. Some of them thought I was just some uppity whippersnapper, but when they heard me put my angle on things, most of them—*all* of them, really—began to pay attention. I do remember when I was in my early teens that God really started *talking to* me. Not out loud, but inside my head," he said.

"Inside your *head*? You know how that sounds?"

"Yeah, kind of crazy, I guess. It's like, I had learned all the ritual prayers in my tradition and knew all the ins and outs of the Jewish religion. But I came to the point that I just started talking to him as if he was standing right next to me; you know, having a conversation with him. And there were other things happening to me at that time; like I remember when I came across a dead bird by the side of the road. I had no inkling about making it live again or whatever, but I did pick it up and cradle the body in my hands. Within five seconds the bird came back to life and flew away. It scared the *shit* out of me!"

I knew it would me. "So did you start experimenting with that power you had?"

"Yeah, I did. A few small animals and minor injuries to my friends, like cuts and bruises and stuff. I was afraid it was going to my head, but God always gave me a sense of peace about it, so I kept my eyes open for any opportunity to do stuff. And it made people happy to see it or experience it. Probably made the small animals and birds happy too."

I took a quick glance at Poppy curled up by my feet under the table. She didn't appear to be listening.

"By the time I was fourteen, I felt like I knew the Jewish scriptures as well as the religious leaders at the temple. I spent literally hours and hours discussing passages from the Hebrew scriptures and debating different interpretations with them. I was starting to realize that *something* was happening to me. By the time I started traveling with my brothers James and Jude, all of us between the ages of thirteen to sixteen, I began to realize that *maybe* I just might be Messiah."

"*Christ . . .*," I muttered in astonishment.

"Yes, the Christ. I'll tell you a bit about what happened to me between the ages of fourteen and my late twenties. Those were really my formative years. I learned much of what I ended up teaching during my ministry because of what I learned during those years of traveling throughout Egypt and India. When we finally came back home to Nazareth, I began teaching the good news about God and his Kingdom, after being baptized by my cousin John. But just because I finally knew who I was and what God wanted me to teach doesn't mean that my disciples understood. I mean, they eventually saw me heal many people and started to catch the drift of my teaching, so they were inclined to think that maybe I *was* the promised Messiah who was to come to establish God's Kingdom on earth. They expected me to lead a revolt against the Romans and sit on the throne of David in the temple, ruling the land, and ultimately the world, with compassion and bringing peace to all the nations." He paused for a moment and said, "But that didn't happen—at least not the way they thought it would."

Joshua reached for my pack of cigarettes and lit one up. I followed his lead.

"By the time we arrived back in Nazareth, I was twenty-nine. There was a palpable *longing* inside me. When I heard that my cousin John was preaching a message of repentance and baptizing people in the Jordan River, I knew in my heart that God wanted me to be baptized by him. He was hesitant to baptize me at first, but I just stood by him in the water and talking quietly to him until he finally did. After I came up out of the water, the masses along the river were going nuts! I asked my brother James what the crowd was all abuzz about. He told me with great excitement that when I was under water, a booming voice was heard saying, 'This is my chosen one; today I have appointed him as my messenger!' I knew right then that God had anointed me to be his messenger, his 'son,' and that I was to start proclaiming the Kingdom of God message that I had learned in my travels: Don't be anxious or afraid of anything in this life, including your own death. Try to live life to the fullest every day, trusting in God for all your needs, and treat others the way you want to be treated, always standing up against injustice."

I tried to imagine Joshua being baptized and the voice coming out of the sky. I couldn't. I've never heard the audible voice of God in my experience, although that doesn't say much about my own faith, I guess.

He reached across the kitchen table and put his hand on my arm. Whew, I could feel something—some kind of power or electricity, or *something*.

"That's when I knew that God had chosen me to preach the message of the Kingdom of God. I felt it inside me, even though I didn't hear the voice from the sky. That's when it all began."

Chapter Twenty-Seven

I did a quick mental review before continuing on with the interview.

I got up to get the pot of coffee and refilled our cups. I went back to the kitchen table where Joshua and Joseph were sitting quietly. They watched me intently as I moved back into position.

Joshua said, "Think about what we're doing together, Rog. Here I am answering your questions so that I can set the record straight about why God appointed me to spread his message about the Kingdom of God so many years ago."

"Yeah, I hear you, Josh. What I want to ask you now is—"

"No," he said. "We need to make another trip first."

"Another trip?" I wondered. So I asked him straight out, "Are we going back in time again?" I was pretty excited about the prospect of going back.

"Yeah," he answered. "We're going back."

Chapter Twenty-Eight

I thought excitedly, "Here we go again!" This time I was ready.

The three of us took our positions in the center of the living room. Without a word, we held hands and waited for that wild wind to blow and take us back.

Nothing.

We waited for a good five minutes; Joshua was getting nervous, it seemed to me. He looked up at the ceiling in silence for a few seconds and then said, "I need a few minutes alone. Can I use the spare room for a minute, Rog?"

"No problem," I answered.

Joshua got up from his chair and kind of shuffled down the hallway to the spare room. After about five minutes (it seemed a lot longer as Joseph and I just sat there in silence, kind of ignoring each other), Joshua came back to the kitchen table and said, "Okay, everything is cool."

"Everything is cool," I thought. I couldn't help but ask, "So what did your Dad say?"

There was a situation he had to deal with was all he said.

Oh, well, I didn't want to pry into what Joshua might be saying to his Dad or what the "situation" was that his Dad had been dealing with. None of my business, I figured.

So we took our places in the living room again, held hands, and within seconds there was a *swooshing* sound as the wind developed suddenly and filled the room.

"AAhhhhh!" I shouted as we lifted off the ground, through the roof of my apartment building (seeing a few families on our way through their apartments), and continued into the sky.

That's all I remembered.

Chapter Twenty-Nine

I came to just when my body thumped down onto the ground. "Here we are," I thought to myself. I did my inventory thing and, aside from a few aches and pains, realized that everything was working.

"So where am I this time?" I wondered. I hazarded a look around, and it was dark. "Must be night," I thought. I was right. I must have been in some sort of field, but I could see lights off in the distance. Lots of fires burning brightly and maybe some huge lanterns, it seemed to me. I felt around in the dark, crawling on my knees, and my hand bumped into something hard. I knocked on it. My eyes were starting to get used to the darkness, and I realized I was knocking on a human head; Joshua's head, it turned out.

He got to his knees, wiped his eyes with his hands, and said, "Good deal. We made it."

But where was Joseph? Our eyes were fully adjusted to the dark, but we didn't see anybody else in the field we found ourselves in.

We could see the lights of what I considered to be a pretty big town, more like a city, really, off in the distance. I estimated that we were about two miles away. We started treading carefully through the fresh camel dung in the field.

Splooch! I heard as I stepped squarely into a fresh pile. "*Yikes*!" I thought as I looked down and saw camel shit creeping up over the sides of my sandals. "How am I supposed to get this stuff off?" I thought.

"You can't," Joshua said, trying not to break into laughter. He was smiling a big smile, and his eyes were sparkling in the firelight from the nearby city.

After about thirty minutes, we arrived at the wall that surrounded the city.

"Where are we?"

"Jerusalem. I need to tell you something before we go any further. I'm supposed to be dead."

Hmmm, he looked all right to me. I waited for him to continue.

"Today is Sunday, two days after I was crucified. My followers are all in hiding, scared o death that they might be arrested by the Romans, or worse, captured by the Pharisees."

The Pharisees were the Jewish teachers of the Torah, which are the laws to be followed in the Hebrew scriptures. They were highly regarded among orthodox Jews at the time. I remembered from Bible college that Jesus, that is, Joshua, had had quite a few run-ins with the Pharisees when he was here before. He wasn't a big fan.

"Here's what's going to happen. This morning we're going to observe."

"What!" I exclaimed. "I don't get it." I was almost apoplectic.

"I'm bringing you with me for the greatest single event in human history—when God raised me from the dead and I appeared to my followers. You'll have to pretend you're an angel. Just try not to say much and do what I say," he added.

Holy *shit*! I was supposed to be an angel? And I'm actually *with* Jesus Christ on the first Easter morning?

I decided to take him at his word and just follow his lead.

Instead of entering the city at the gate in the wall surrounding it, Joshua headed toward the nearby hills, about half an hour's walk from the city walls. The sun was just about to make its appearance on the horizon. We came to some rocky crags about halfway up the side of one of the hills. There were a bunch of holes in the rocky hillside—almost like caves. Some of them had huge rocks covering the entrances, and carefully sculpted rocks in front of some. Graves. We were carefully making our way through a large cemetery. We made it to the top of the pretty high, rocky hill just as the sun was breaking the horizon. We started down on the other side. By the time half of the sun could be seen on the horizon, we had made it back down about halfway on the other side of the hill, facing away from Jerusalem. There in front of us was an open tomb. There was a huge rock off to the side, as if someone had just moved it away from the entrance. We were standing about twenty yards away—half-hidden behind a huge rock and some sparse bushes. There, kneeling by the open tomb, was a woman. Even from such a distance I could tell she was severely distraught. Not just that she was crying, but she was also wailing.

Omigod! It dawned on me. That must be Mary Magdalene coming to check out the tomb of—Joshua! Jesus! The Son of God! It was Easter morning, and the sun had finally freed itself from the horizon.

Joshua put his finger to his lips. "Be very quiet," he whispered to me in English. "You're about to see something special happen."

I crouched down a bit farther behind the rock. I had a clear view of whatever was about to happen.

Chapter Thirty

As we watched, she got down on her knees. I sensed somebody else was there! Mary did too. Still on her knees, she craned her neck around so that she could see who it was. But she couldn't see. Her eyes were flooded with tears, and her nose was all runny. She tried to blink away the tears and focused on a human form.

The rest is history.

"Who are you?" she asked the figure, looking tearfully in his direction.

The figure didn't respond. I immediately noticed that the man looked a lot like—Joshua! I turned to glance at Joshua, and he shushed me with a finger to his lips.

"Please," she begged through her tears, "tell me what you've done with my Lord's body."

We could see from our vantage point that the stone was rolled away from the cave tomb. But where was the Roman guard whom Pilate had ordered to make sure that no one came and took away his body?

Joshua was transfixed. For the second time today, he was seeing himself. I couldn't begin to imagine what was going on in his mind.

As we watched from our hiding place, Jesus of Nazareth stepped toward Mary and said, "Miriam. Don't be afraid. It's me, Yeshua."

"What's with the Miriam thing?" I wondered. Then I remembered they were speaking in Aramaic. I was still thinking in English, like the last time, but I understood everything that was being said.

"Yeshua?" she asked tentatively.

"*Yeshua*? How can . . . what . . . ," she stammered. "Is it really *you*?" she finally got out.

"Yes," he said. "It's really me. As I told you and the others would happen before I was crucified, God has raised me from the dead. I'm *baaack*!" he said in his best Jack Nicholson voice.

She couldn't speak. She just scrambled to her knees, ran the few short steps toward Jesus, and flew into his arms. He held her up, and she wrapped her legs around him. She was kissing him all over his face and head. Finally she locked lips with his, and they remained like that for . . . for at least thirty seconds!

I didn't know what to do. Should I look away and give them some privacy? I couldn't. The sight was so emotional that I just stood there, my eyes glued on the two of them.

Joshua, too, was frozen in place. I sneaked a glance at his face. Tears were streaming down his cheeks. His shoulders sagged.

Miriam eventually disentangled herself from her Lord, stood back, and stared at him. Just stared. No tears, just eyes glistening and a wonderful smile on her face.

"Where have you *been*?" she said. "We all knew you were dead, but I remembered what you said to us: that you would come back to life after a few days. Is this what you were talking about?" she asked tentatively.

"It is," Jesus the Nazarene said. "This was God's plan all along—that I would be appointed by him to teach and show people how to live in communion with God and each other and then die so that he could raise me from the dead, to show everyone what he does with every human being."

Looking around Jesus asked, "Where is everyone? I kind of figured that the whole gang would be here at my grave to see what happened."

"We're all so afraid," Miriam said. "We're afraid the Roman soldiers and the Pharisees would band together to gather us up and condemn all of us to death for being your followers. We scattered and hid in the houses of some of your secret devotees in the city. What do you want me to do, Lord? Should I go tell the rest that you're alive again?"

Jesus seemed to reflect on her question before answering, "Yes. Go tell them you've seen me and to stay in the upper room until I come to see them. I won't be long."

With that she embraced him again, this time giving him a peck on the cheek and then started making her way carefully back up the hill and down again on the other side.

"She can hardly wait to tell them," I thought.

I looked back at Jesus to see if—what? He was nowhere to be seen! I looked over at Joshua, both of us by this time up on our feet.

"Where'd he go?" I asked.

Joshua smiled and said, "I'm right here."

Really? Had this really just happened? I always felt like I had an open mind and stuff, but I was totally flummoxed. I didn't know what else to say.

After a few minutes of flummoxing, I turned to Joshua and asked, "What do we do now?"

"Follow me," he said.

So I did.

Chapter Thirty-One

He led me back up the hill and started down on the Jerusalem side. We stopped about halfway down, making our way carefully through the rocky hillside. I noticed tons of graves in the side of the hill, some covered with huge rocks and some not.

"Must be waiting for customers," I thought.

Joshua picked a secluded spot surrounded by sparse trees. There he told us to gather some moss and branches so he could make a fire. I was looking forward to this! "How long would it take to start a flame?" I wondered.

Not long. When he had placed some small twigs and some moss into a pile, he reached deftly into a pocket of his robe and pulled out a BIC lighter.

"What the . . . ?" I thought. "That doesn't seem right. Is this how it really happened when it really happened? Or was it really happening *right now*?"

"It's a little different," he said, reading my thoughts. "We're here so that you can *experience* what happened on Easter morning, not to fiddle over the details."

Soon he had the fire going, and he had somehow produced (from where?) a filleted fish. Filleted? Oh, well, I was getting hungry, and there's nothing like fish cooked over a campfire. Each of us had long sticks with a huge chunk of fish skewered to each one, holding it in the fire until my mouth started watering from the aroma. I had found two small flat rocks when we were gathering the wood for the fire, which we used as plates. I took the fish off my stick and put it on my rock. Joshua did the same.

I took my first bite, and oh, it was *so good*! We munched away noisily for a few minutes before Joshua looked at me and asked, "Are you thirsty?"

I was. I always had to have a glass of milk or water or *something* when I was eating. I guess I just figured that I would have to go without way out here on the hillside.

But no. Joshua reached back into his robe and pulled out a medium-sized wineskin fat with liquid. He tossed it over to me and said, "Have some wine."

"Have some wine?" I thought? "It was just after sunrise!" Still, I needed something to wash the fish down with, so I grabbed the wineskin, opened the top spout, and had a long haul.

"Omigod!" I thought. The wine slithered down my throat without any burning at all and no acidic aftertaste. "What's up with *this*?" I wondered.

"It's an 1876 Bordeaux," he said. "One of my favorites."

I was . . . I was impressed, I guess. What else was in that magic robe of his? Maybe a Mars bar for dessert?

"No," he answered, "That's about it. Just thought we might need some refreshment while we can. It could be a long day."

I took another healthy swig from the wineskin and tossed back to Joshua. He took another long drink and snapped the cap back into place.

"We'll save a bit for later. I have this feeling we're going to need it," he said. "This is the most momentous occasion in human history, Rog, what we're experiencing today. My Dad wanted you to actually experience what happened on this first Easter morning."

Joshua got up and started to scatter the fire.

"Only *you* can prevent forest fires," he said in his best Smokey the Bear voice.

"How many imitations did the Son of God have?" I wondered.

"Tons of them, Rog. I've been practicing them for a long time."

"Really?" I thought. I tried to imagine God's Son practicing different celebrity voices. I couldn't.

With the fire out, we started trudging down the rocky hillside toward Jerusalem. For some reason I was getting that bad feeling again in the pit of my stomach. I told myself to get it together.

Chapter Thirty-Two

We both had our hoodies up as we entered the city of Jerusalem through one of its many guarded gates. I wasn't anywhere near drunk, but I did feel warm and relaxed. It was a good feeling. As soon as we were within the walls of the city, Joshua stopped and pulled us aside into a narrow alleyway. He sat down on the ground next to a blind beggar beseeching the odd person who might venture into the alley. He heard us sit down next to him and asked, "Do you have any coins for me? As you can see, I'm blind, and I'm barely making it." I looked at him closely. He was a young man but garbed in a dirty robe and had an out-of-control bush for a beard.

"How old are you?" I asked.

"I don't know," he said. "I used to have a beautiful wife and three kids until I was blinded years ago. Now I'm just waiting to die, I guess. I've lost everything."

I was so curious to hear his story about who blinded him and why, but Joshua beat me to the punch.

"Look, man," he said quickly and unthinkingly, "we're right in the middle of something so we kind of need you to vamoose."

"Kind of rude," I thought, but I kept my mouth shut.

Suddenly Joshua looked over at the guy again and said, "Sorry about that, man. How about this: close your eyes for ten seconds, open them, and you'll have your sight back."

I was dumbfounded.

The blind beggar did what Joshua told him to do and, ten seconds later, opened his eyes.

"I can see!" he whispered loudly. "I can't believe it! I can see!" he repeated.

Then he added a caveat, "Can you add some color?" he asked, looking straight at Joshua.

Joshua glanced toward me with a "Really?" look on his face and then said to the guy, "Sure."

The no-longer-blind beggar said, "Holy shit! This is too good to be true! Please, sir, tell me what I can do to repay you?"

Joshua hesitated. "Go to the temple and wash your face in holy water—and don't tell anyone about me!" he added emphatically. "Just tell people that you woke up this morning with sight. Now go find your wife and kids, if you can, and vamoose."

Was Joshua telling the beggar to lie?

"Just a little white one," he whispered to me in English. "Now stay quiet."

The beggar stood up, stared intently at Joshua, and said, "Surely you are a son of the most high God!"

Then he left.

"Pretty close to the truth," I said.

Joshua nodded. "Yeah," he said. "Pretty damn close."

Chapter Thirty-Three

We were both still sitting in the narrow alley when he turned to me and said, "So are you ready for this?"

"For *what*?" I asked.

"For my first visit to my followers since I was crucified," he said. "I'm not exactly sure what's going to happen, but it should be pretty exciting—and a bit weird."

"But what about . . . well, *you*? Like, where is Jesus of Nazareth?" I asked with more-than-a-little confusion.

"Not to worry, Rog. My Dad has it all figured out. Ready?"

"Okay," I said. "Let's do it."

Chapter Thirty-Four

But it didn't turn out quite the way I expected. Instead of making our way through the streets, Joshua told me to take his hand. Still in the alley, I took his hand as he looked down and started mumbling quietly.

"He must be praying," I thought.

He was.

Suddenly a small whirlwind lifted Joshua and I up from the ground into the sky. This time I kept my eyes open and tried to stay calm. "What the heck is going on?" I thought. But I kind of had a hint that he was taking us to see his disciples where they were hiding in fear for their lives.

We landed softly at the door of a second-story room, presumably somewhere in Jerusalem. I was suitably impressed with this mode of travel. I started to tell him that, but he stopped me by saying, "Take my hand again, Rog, and try to prepare yourself. You're going to walk right through this door."

"Really?" I thought. I figured maybe *he* could walk through solid objects, but I was pretty sure I'd just get a bump on the head.

But I was wrong.

In an instant we were inside the upper room, standing right by the door. I looked around and saw seven, no eight, guys in various poses of sitting and standing, talking quietly but excitedly to each other. And, of course, there was Miriam seated in the middle. She had obviously told them that she had seen Jesus alive outside of his tomb. Now they were trying to figure out what she was on, I guess.

But she wasn't "on" anything, I knew. She had seen the risen Jesus. He had talked with her, embraced her, and kissed her. He was alive and real.

"Ahem," Joshua said from the door.

All heads turned to the sound, and all eyes focused on Joshua. Then all hell broke loose.

The eight men started crowding around him as he moved further into the room. They clawed at his clothes, touched his hands, and ruffled his hair (I could tell he didn't like that, but he didn't stop them). Then they took turns one by one embracing him. He would hold each disciple tightly for a good ten seconds before moving on to the next. The room was a cacophony of sounds: excited voices, joyful crying, exclamations of "Praise God!" and "Holy *shit*!" filled the air. It was pretty cool, truth be told.

No one approached me. I don't think anyone even *saw* me yet. It didn't bother me. I was content to just take it all in—the excitement, the hugging, the teary smiles. It was—well, you had to be there.

Joshua settled in and sat down on a well-crafted chair. Miriam came and sat down on a coarse pillow on the floor beside him. The other disciples gathered in front of him, some sitting and some standing.

Me, I was still standing by the door. When everyone was settled, Joshua called over to me to come and stand by his chair. Every head turned to me with whispers of "Who's *that*?" and "I didn't see him over there."

Then Peter spoke to the rest of the disciples, saying, "It's Rahj!" Then he turned to me. "Welcome back, Rahj. Good to see you again," he said a bit uncomfortably. He and the others still really didn't know who I was or what I was doing hanging out with the Messiah. Especially in this situation where they were seeing their Master in the flesh for the first time after seeing him horribly killed on the Roman cross.

Joshua walked over and stood by his chair, he looked at his disciples, and said, "Rahj is an angel of the Lord." He lied again. "Please give him the respect that you show me."

They all looked at me, some with envy. But not Miriam.

That seemed to do the trick. I guess they just figured I was some angel whom Jesus liked hanging out with.

They quickly turned their attention back toward Joshua. He started to talk to them in a quiet voice. His basic theme was, "Don't be afraid. I *told* you I would be brought back to life. Now you know that everything I taught you was the truth. That's what will happen to all of *you* after you die. So don't be afraid."

I sat stunned along with the rest of the disciples. Only Miriam remained silent.

Suddenly there was a cacophony of voices.

"When are you coming back to establish God's Kingdom here on earth?" was the gist of most of the questions.

He looked at them all and said, "I don't know. Only God knows for sure. "

Everyone began talking at the same time.

Joshua hushed them and said, "But remember, unless you become as a little child in your faith, you may not be able to enter God's Kingdom."

That's when all hell broke loose again.

"What do you mean?" and "How can I become a child again?" and "Really?" Everyone wanted to know what the heck he was talking about.

But the important thing is that they were talking to a guy who had been horribly crucified less than two days ago. The excited talk eventually came back to that fact.

Peter took the lead, stood up, and turned around to the rest of the disciples.

"He's here!" he said. "And now we know that everything he said and did comes from God, for God has raised him from the dead!" The others went nuts.

While Peter was talking to the other disciples, Joshua looked up at me from where he was sitting and whispered to me, "We're outta here." Then he leaned down toward Miriam and said the same thing.

We all three held hands together while the disciples were busy with Peter, and *poof*!

We were outta there.

Chapter Thirty-Five

I recognized the place where we had come to a soft rest. It was in the secret place outside of Capernaum, hidden so that no one could see us from the road.

When I realized where we were, I was a bit stunned. I asked Joshua, "Where's . . . well, where's *you*? Like, your disciples saw us in the upper room, but that was you, not . . . do you see where I'm going with this, Josh?"

"Yeah, he'll be a bit confused about it, I'm sure, but he'll figure it out. It's my Dad who must be having quite the laugh with this whole thing."

Joshua sat down, and we sat with him. Miriam was actually half-draped over him, playing with his ears and hair. I watched as she snuggled up and kissed him for what seemed like a minute, at least. They kissed passionately.

It was an awkward moment, at least for me. I began to wonder what I was supposed to be doing.

He reflected for a moment and said, "I want you to have the opportunity to talk to Miriam, to Mary. I want you to get to know her—her hopes and dreams and, of course, her secrets. I think that getting to know her a bit will give you a better idea about what we're doing in your apartment—finding out what I'm really like and what we're trying to do together. Can you do that for me?" he asked.

I didn't need much encouragement to spend some time with Miriam. She certainly wasn't hard to look at.

"Sure," I said. "I'd really like that. Where are you going to be while we're chatting?" I asked.

"Not here. I have some important visits to make as long as we're here. I'll be back in a couple of hours."

I started to think about our precious interview time and then quickly remembered that the hours spent here were only a few minutes in the twenty-first century. That helped to relieve my mind.

"Okay," I said, "let's do it. Can you leave us a bit of fish and the rest of the wine, though?"

"Sure thing, Rog."

He reached into his fancy robe and took out the wineskin. It was bulging. *Hmmm*, how did *that* happen? Then he reached behind him ("Did he have a big pocket back there?" I wondered), and took out a huge loaf of flatbread, crammed chock full of nuts, cheese, wild berries, and small pieces of chicken. "Yeah," I thought, "I think this will work out just fine."

Chapter Thirty-Six

I turned around to thank Joshua, but he was nowhere to be seen. I hadn't even heard anything. He was gone.

Miriam was standing a few feet away. She was looking down but had a wonderfully cute smile on her face. She looked at me and said, "The Lord has told me so much about you, Roger. I can hardly wait to share some things with you."

We sat cross-legged on the ground, facing each other. As she looked me in the eye, she reached out the short distance and took my left hand. She said, "Thank you so much for doing this with me, Roger." She continued, "Yeshua has told me all about you. He really likes you, Roger. He loves you, of course, because it's in his DNA to love."

"DNA?" I thought. "She knows about *DNA*?"

"But it's easy to *love* somebody; it's much harder to *like* somebody."

"Yep," I thought. "She definitely had hung out with Joshua a lot. She even *sounded* like him."

She broke into my thoughts, "Yeshua has taught me *so much* over the past three years. And now he's been raised from the dead by his Father. I *knew* he'd come back. I just *knew* it."

Man, I wish I had that kind of faith. Maybe I would after this experience with Joshua. I wanted to ask her about some of his secret teachings that he had told her and not the other disciples.

"Yes," she interjected my thoughts, "I will tell you about some of those secrets."

Omigod! Could she read my mind too? The very thought made me *so nervous.*

"I can't read minds," she said. "Well, maybe Yeshua's every now and then because we're so close, but I am very sensitive to people's expressions and inner language. Would you like to ask me questions, or would you prefer that I free-form about those secrets?"

Free-form? Isn't that the expression I used when talking with Joshua in my apartment?

"Yeah, Miriam, I'd like it if you shared some things that *you* think are important," I replied.

"Okay, let's start with the Big Picture. How about this: we are not alone!"

What? Was there someone lurking around in the bush or something?

"No, no"—she laughed—"I mean Yeshua told me that we're not alone in the universe. There are millions and millions of planets in the universe with intelligent life; most of them very much like human beings in appearance and thinking. And not just intelligent life forms. There are billions of other plants and animals and . . . ," she hesitated. "The universe is teeming with life. And Yeshua told me that God's not done creating. In fact, he'll *never* be done."

I was just listening—*really* listening. I didn't even have to ask any questions.

She continued, "There are billions of spiritual beings too. We can't see them in our earthly bodies, but they are all around us. We all have spiritual beings who help us through this life. Yeshua told me that boredom will never even enter our minds in the afterlife. It will be so stimulating and exciting all the time. We'll be involved in teaching people from other planets about what it was like living and fighting for our lives on earth, visiting and interacting with billions of other beings from other planets, being part of God's creative team as he continues to dream up other fantastic things to make. Yeshua went on and on about it, but I hope that satisfies you and alleviates any fears you might have about being 'bored' in the life to come."

It did. But before I had time to ask other questions about this life, my mind veered in the direction of this one, especially about Yeshua and his relationship with this mystery woman.

"So when did you first meet Joshua, and how did you come to be his soul mate?" I asked.

"When Yeshua started his public teaching," she began, "word got around fast. He was actually healing people from serious physical and mental illnesses. Can you imagine, Roger? I had to see this man. I come from a very wealthy family, so money has never been a problem. When I followed the crowd out to the countryside one day, I saw him from a distance. I had to get closer. So I made my way through the crowd until I was right in front of him. I sat right at his feet and gazed up at him as he taught."

She stopped for a minute, remembering, I think. Then she continued, "Then, in the middle of a sentence, his eyes caught mine. His eyes blazed, and I immediately got the feeling that he *knew* me, really *knew* me. In those brief seconds that we maintained eye contact, he stopped speaking. In those brief seconds, I felt all sorts of things. I knew immediately that he *loved* me; I got the feeling there was an instantaneous love connection—almost like love at first sight. And I sensed a deep *compassion* in him, as if he understood everything about me and *knew* everything about me. Tears flooded my eyes. And his eyes. The crowd started murmuring, wondering why he had stopped speaking. He exuded compassion and empathy and love and understanding. I had to meet him—to talk to him and touch him. I just *had* to."

I was enraptured.

She went on, "So I did. After he was finished teaching, I waited patiently for the throng of people surrounding him to thin out. Then, with only his closest followers around him, I stood up from where I was sitting, took a few steps toward him, and the disciples parted. There we were, just me and him. The rest of his disciples had slowly drifted away, and we were alone. I knew he had somehow made that happen."

Miriam stopped for a moment to wipe away some tears with the back of her hand.

Then she said, "He reached out both of his hands, and I placed my hands in his. Immediately he drew me close to his body. I could feel his heart beating wildly inside of his chest.

Mine, too, was palpitating. He kissed the top of my head, then my nose, and moved down to my lips. We hadn't yet spoken a word, and he was kissing me passionately! After a few seconds, I disengaged my lips from his mouth. He looked at me and said, 'Miriam. You are the love of my life.'"

I . . . I didn't want her to stop, so I didn't say anything.

She went on, "I knew it too. He was the One. Not just for the people, but for *me*. The disciples were murmuring among themselves from a distance, having witnessed the whole scene. I sensed that they weren't happy. One of them looked at me with a disgusting gaze and whispered something to the rest of them. I knew right then that our fledgling relationship was going to undergo much turmoil, mostly from his closest followers. But nothing could deter me. He was the One."

My mouth must have been hanging open. I just wanted her to keep talking.

So she did.

"We began hanging out together wherever he decided to go," she said. "I told him that I wanted to help pay for food and lodging and clothes—anything he and his disciples needed. There were other women, too, who began following him, and many of them, too, offered him money for traveling expenses. But I never felt intimidated or jealous. I knew that I truly was his muse, the love of his life. *I felt it so strongly*. Whenever we could, we would secret ourselves off from the others and kiss passionately, holding on to each other for dear life. It was *so* wonderful! He would sweetly entwine his tongue with mine. I would playfully brush the back of my hand against his hardness. He often let out a passionate sigh when I did that. After a few times of being physically intimate, I *so* longed for him to be inside me. I told him so. I could feel the breath going out of him as he sighed and said, 'Oh, Miriam! How I would so love to marry you! But I must stay focused on my Father's business. Will you stay by my side even though we never get married?'

"'Yes, my Lord, you know I will.' And I did."

"Joshua is a lucky man," I said.

"Yes, he is," she replied without guile. "But I am the luckiest person in the history of humankind!"

Chapter Thirty-Seven

We spent hours together, her talking and me listening. I would ask questions when they arose in my mind, but that was rare. Mostly she kept telling me about what Joshua had told her, unbelievable secret things. I felt I had to get them into this memoir. But I couldn't. She told me that it was enough that I knew these secrets. But I couldn't share them with the world. I was both disappointed and ecstatic. I really didn't want to have to tell them to the world. Then they would no longer be secrets. But that she, and by extension Joshua, trusted me with them was a gift I would forever treasure.

Suddenly there was a loud *whooshing* sound, and Joshua was back.

"Hey, guys, how's it going? Ready to wrap things up here?" he asked.

I wasn't, but I knew it was time. There was still an interview to finish back at my apartment. But I treasured what Miriam had told me and made a mental note to tell people about my conversation with her—as much as I could share, anyway.

Miriam looked up from where she was sitting and made eye contact with Joshua. They smiled that knowing "only between lovers" kind of smile. Joshua said, "Okay, Rog, just give me a few minutes alone with Miriam, and we'll head back."

Miriam scrambled to her feet, obviously aware of what was going on in the future.

I said good-bye to Miriam, hugging her closely.

She turned and hugged Joshua briefly and left, treading her way down the hillside until she was out of sight.

Joshua turned to me and asked, "So how did it go, Rog?"

"It was perfect, Josh. Now I know—I have a better sense of who you are and *why* you are."

"We'll talk about that, Rog. Ready to go?"

Chapter Thirty-Eight

After Joshua and I crash-landed on the balcony (again), we briefly checked ourselves out and took up residence in the living room. I sat on the couch, and Joshua took the overstuffed leather chair.

Suddenly the thought popped into my mind: where was Joseph? We had spent a good six hours in first-century Jerusalem on the first Easter day, and it was just dawning on me that Joseph hadn't been there. I asked Joshua about where he might be.

"No idea," he said. "The last I remember is that we were all holding hands waiting to go back."

"Me too," I said. "Should we somehow go look for him?" Not that I was concerned all that much. But I was curious.

"No," Joshua said. "He'll be back. I'm sure of it."

"Okay, then," I said. "Should we get back to the interview?"

"Yes, let's do that," he answered.

So we did.

Chapter Thirty-Nine

The last thing Joseph remembered was they were taking another trip back in time. He wasn't exactly sure where they were headed, but it entered his mind that he really didn't want to go. That was the thought in his mind when the whirlwind started in the apartment. He just wished he could spend some time with his kin instead.

He got his wish.

When he landed in the heavenly realm, he immediately felt at home. "Well, it *is* my home," he thought. When the Son of God was on earth back in the day, Joseph remembered how he tried to get across the idea of the Kingdom of God to his obstinate disciples. He would try to compare the Kingdom of God with things they might understand, like a mustard seed falling into the ground and dying and then springing up into a huge plant—or how the Kingdom of God is like a farmer gathering in his harvest. Or it's like a monkey's paw, or *whatever*. His disciples just didn't get it. Secretly, Joseph always thought that he could have done a better job of it than Jesus did of explaining it, but he would never *say*, or even *think*, such a thing when he was around him.

Joseph glanced down the way a bit and saw a few of his friends standing around a makeshift fire and making small talk. Angels were a strange lot, but he was glad he *was* one. From his experiences with human types on earth, he thanked the Presence every day that he wasn't one of *them*. He'd only had one small assignment on earth in the span of his existence, at least before now, and it had creeped him out big-time. Humans were so—full of themselves. Angels could be a tad bit self-absorbed at times too, but *nothing* like humans.

But he really liked Rog. They had bonded in the psych ward back on earth, and he was the first human whom Joseph had actually spent time with—talking, playing chess, smoking in the bathroom, and now at his apartment as he interviewed Jesus.

He could tell that Rog was changing. The Lord seemed to have that effect on everyone he interacted with, both back in the day and up to the present. Even though he was a human being, he now knew how devastated he was being estranged from his daughter Alison. He could palpably *feel* the emotions that Rog had toward her, and it made Joseph sad that they were not on speaking terms. Rog *wanted* to be, but his daughter was just too angry and confused about why he tried to kill himself for that to happen. Joseph decided then and there that he was going to do anything in his power to bring them together again.

Joseph understood and spoke a multitude of languages used in different places around the universe. He just had a knack for it, it seemed. Most angels had at least a rudimentary understanding of many of them, but Joseph was conversationally more fluent in them than any other angel he knew personally. There were billions of angels, all with different names. He often wondered how the Presence could really know each and every one of his creations intimately, but he did. He was God, after all, and Joseph understood that no creature, angel or otherwise, could hope to know his mind.

Joseph drew closer to his buddies who were hanging out together. Only Joseph knew where the Lord was at the moment, and he wasn't about to let his friends know that he knew.

But they already did.

How did word of his latest assignment leak out? He was sworn to secrecy by the Presence himself about this assignment. But he could hear the exclamations coming from the half dozen or so angels gathered together as he was about to step up and join them.

"There he is!" he heard one angel say excitedly.

"We've *got* to find out more from him," said another.

The others nodded in agreement. Joseph felt a swelling in his chest. "Pride?" he wondered. He figured it was.

Angels, too, were made in the image of God, so they were capable of experiencing the whole gamut of emotions and attributes that God did: love, compassion, empathy, loyalty, humility, being of service to others, and so on, as well as emotions such as anger and pride. The difference between angels and human types, though, was that angels knew the limits.

"Hey, guys," Joseph said to the group, "what's shakin'?"

Arroyo, one of his best friends, spoke for the rest of them. "We're just so *proud* of you, Joe, and *envious,* if truth be told. From the sounds of it, you're on the assignment of your life!"

Joseph felt light-headed. He didn't realize that his assignment would be considered so unique. Come to think of it, though, it *was*. Very few angels had ever been assigned to accompany Jesus in his travels. It happened on occasion, but it was rare.

"Yeah, it *is* quite the assignment," Joseph said, trying to sound nonchalant.

"So what are you doing here?" Arroyo asked. "And where's the Lord? Aren't you supposed to be helping him?"

"Hmmm," Joseph thought. "How do I answer *that* question?"

He'd always been taught to tell the truth. All angels were taught that right from the beginning, so it was almost impossible for him to lie. He considered it but shut the idea out.

"I needed a break, guys. It was getting pretty intense there on earth with the guy Jesus and his Dad chose to interview Jesus, so I thought I'd drop by for a bit and hang out with my friends."

They understood, kind of. Like, even if he spent a few hours getting some respite from his assignment, it would only be a few minutes in earth time. They knew that too.

The matter settled, his friends started peppering him with questions about how his assignment was going. He answered them all as best he could, telling them about the human, Rog: how they met, what was happening in his apartment, and about the trip back in time. He told them that not all humans were stupid, that Rog was a good guy even though he wasn't an angel, and that Joseph's opinion of human types was changing the more he hung out with him.

After about an hour, everyone seemed satisfied. As a group they were just happy to have some new stories to tell other angels.

Joseph told them that he had to get back anyway, so they said their good-byes and went their individual ways.

Joseph loved the heavenly realm. There were endless exciting things to do and see and experience, tons of friends to hang out with, no pain or threat of the thing that human types seemed so scared of: *death.*

It was time to get back, he figured. He had needed this respite from the earth and the interview situation. He felt refreshed, and he resolved to go back to the apartment and pick up where he had left off with Jesus and Rog.

So he did.

Chapter Forty

Joshua and I were about to get back into interview mode when we heard a loud *thump* out on the balcony.

Joshua and I looked at each other and said at the same time, "Joseph's back."

He limped into the living room from the balcony, rubbing the side of his head.

"Hey, guys," he said, trying to sound nonchalant. "Where'd you guys go?"

Joshua was amused. "You know exactly where we went, Joe. The question is: Where were *you*?"

Joseph looked like a deer trapped in the headlights. "I . . . I, I got my directions wrong," he lied lamely.

Joshua let it go. He knew where Joseph had been and why, but he played along.

"Why don't you tell us where you went and what happened? I want Rog to be sure that he includes your little detour in his memoir."

Joseph had this strained look on his face, probably because of not wanting to share his experiences with us. But what to do? No choice, really, not when the one asking was the Lord.

So he spilled the beans onto my computer's voice recorder.

Chapter Forty-One

After Joseph finished telling us about his little side excursion, and with just a glance at each other, we moved back into position around the kitchen table. Joseph, too, sat down to listen in on the interview. Joshua wasn't upset with him, although he did feel kind of bad that he had lied. But the three of us were back together again, and Joseph settled in comfortably.

After a quick look at my notes, I jumped right in.

"I want to ask you some questions about the Bible. So much of it seems, well, not very relevant to the twenty-first-century human mind. And, let's face it, most of the Bible seems like just so much bull . . ."

"Agreed," Joshua responded, cutting me off. "The Bible is a complicated book. Most Christians believe that God wrote it, but most reasonable people get the fact that all you can really do with the Bible is cherry-pick the good parts and try not to pay much attention to the rest of it."

That made sense to me. When I was in Bible college, the only way I could get anything from the Bible was to do exactly what Joshua was suggesting.

"The Bible tells us how a primitive people saw themselves in relationship to God and their community," he continued. "And the 'God' represented in the Hebrew scriptures, what Christians call the Old Testament, is portrayed pretty much as a petty, vindictive, genocidal, cruel, morally bankrupt god who seems to delight in treachery, deceit, and killing. I'm telling you now very clearly: *God's not like that.*"

"Yeah," I said. "I've always struggled with the portrayal of God in the Old Testament. Sure, most people I know are at least vaguely familiar with the Bible, especially your story. But how many actually pick the damn thing up and *read* it on any kind of regular basis?"

"Right, and why do you think that is?" Joshua asked.

"Because it's long and boring, and God is portrayed as a homicidal psychopath?" I guess I was trying to provoke him a bit, although I wasn't sure why.

"Right," he said, unprovoked. "As I said, what comprises the Bible is merely a collection of ancient manuscripts, written over thousands of years and eventually gathered together. In that sense, the Bible tells us a lot about what people experienced, how they interpreted those experiences, and how they thought God was involved with their lives. But that's about it, Rog. They are ancient writings that tell us what *they* thought about what was going on in their lives and the world around them. Nothing more, nothing less."

"Okay," I said, "I get what you're saying, but how are we supposed to learn about God from Bronze Age people?"

"Well, you can learn a lot from those ancient writings about how people thought and lived back then. But men have always had their agendas, and the Bible is pretty much a product of dominant male thinking."

"Yeah, and the whole male superiority thinking we still see in Christianity today is based on it."

"True, for the most part. The idea that most Christians have that the Bible is the 'Word of God' is loopy. It presents a terribly skewed picture of a god who condones slavery, human trafficking, killing gays, condemning kids who have sex outside of marriage to death; the list goes on. God appointed me to reveal *who he really is*. The Bible really is one big collection of ancient ideas, stories, perspectives, and experiences, but it doesn't have much to do with reality."

"Well, it is good for one thing. I found out years ago that the thin pages are great for rolling cigarettes."

"Yeah, and other substances too, I hear. But the problem is that most Christians put their brains in neutral when thinking about the Bible. Christian leaders, pastors, ministers, and priests teach their respective followers that 'God wrote it. I believe it. That settles it.'"

"I remember hearing that when I was at Bible college. I always thought that sounded like they were throwing their minds away. In my experience, Christians just believe whatever their priests or pastors or ministers tell them to believe."

"That is true, but God chose me to try to put an end to that kind of thinking. He appointed me to proclaim the Kingdom of God and to teach people to use their minds, their *reason,* to separate fact from fiction and to figure out *why* you believe *what* you believe. I came to reveal the mind of God to everyone, both by what I taught and how I lived."

"So did the four Gospel writers who wrote about what you taught and how you lived accurately record what you *really* said and did?"

"No. It's important to keep in mind that the writers of the Gospels pieced together a patchwork of my life and teachings, sometimes exaggerating and even making stuff up to reflect what their respective faith communities were starting to believe about God and me. The writers of the Gospels weren't my disciples. All their knowledge was secondhand and thirdhand. The authors of Matthew and Luke basically copied ninety percent of what was written in the Gospel of Mark, which was written about twenty years earlier, and then added their own material on the basis of what they and their respective faith communities believed. The question is this: Why did they feel the need to change what Mark had written twenty years earlier? Because their respective Christian communities had their own agendas and beliefs. Keep in mind that there were various forms of Christianity in the first and second centuries, all believing that *their* version of Christianity was the only true one."

"Can you give me an example of what you're talking about?" I asked.

"Yeah, I can. Matthew's Gospel reports that, after I had uttered my last breath on the cross, 'A great earthquake shook the land and the veil of the temple was torn from top to bottom.' But how could he know that the veil was torn? Only the high priest was allowed to enter the holiest part of the temple where the veil was, and then only once a year. So we're not talking about any kind of historical accuracy here. The same mythologizing can be found when Matthew reports that hundreds of graves were opened up and bodies of the dead started walking around."

"Like in *The Walking Dead*?" I asked.

"Yeah, and sometimes I think I'm a lot like Daryl . . . The point is that certainly such an event, had it actually occurred, would have been recorded by the other Gospel writers, not to mention recorded in some other Jewish or Roman historical source. But what do we find? Nothing."

"So you're saying that the Gospel writers exaggerated and added their own personal biases to support their particular belief about you?"

"Yes. Keep in mind that there were no printing presses or mass production of documents in those days. Everything had to be copied by scribes. And often the scribes, too, had their own theological perspectives that they wanted to add to the texts they were copying, be it a Gospel or a letter or whatever. New Testament scholars today know all about how the original manuscripts were changed as they were being copied again and again over the decades after they were written. There no longer exist any originals of any New Testament writings, so we have to compare the various differences between the copies of the copies we *do* have. Doing that reveals how and why the documents were changed by the scribes over the decades after my death."

"Did they do it intentionally? I mean, isn't that unethical?"

"There were no copyright laws in those days, and it was a common practice for scribes and copyists to change the meaning of a passage of a manuscript to suit their own theological beliefs. The Bible is replete with contradictions, scientific errors, and falsehoods. The best biblical scholars, textual critics, and historians have discovered and reported on those contradictions and falsehoods, particularly over the past one hundred years or so. Historians and textual critics have written books designed for the average reader about these things. Human reasoning skills continue to evolve, Rog, and here we are in the twenty-first century with our minds continuing to expand and new knowledge being discovered virtually every day. I'm here now to tell you the truth about God's reality."

"Do you have more examples of when the Gospel writers just made stuff up?" I asked.

"Yeah. One of the most well-known passages in the Bible is about the woman caught in adultery. You can find that story in John's Gospel. The Jewish religious authorities dragged her into the middle of the town square so the gathering crowd could stone her to death. As the story goes, I happened along the scene and stopped them from stoning her by asking, 'Let those of you who are without sin cast the first stone.' Then I allegedly took a knee and began writing in the dirt with a pointy rock."

"What did you write?" I asked.

"Man, Rog, you worry me sometimes. I wasn't there! That's an apocryphal story—a made-up story to portray me as a forgiving fellow, I guess."

"Oh, yeah, sorry dude. The thing is, many, many people know that story, and for many it's their favorite story about you. So, anyway, what happened next in the story? Like, I know what happens according to the Bible, but what have you heard over the years?"

"Everyone dropped their rocks and backed away. According to the Bible, I then told the girl caught in adultery, 'Go, child, and sin no more.'"

"Well, it's still a good story, right?"

"Yeah, it is. The only thing is that it never happened. One more example: the story where I allegedly raised Lazarus back to life after he had been dead and in the grave for four days. According to the Bible, most of my disciples were there to witness this astonishing act. Amazingly, the author of the Gospel of John is the only one to record the event. And believe me, if I did have the power to bring people back to life after they died, why not do it for everyone? I always thought, too, that Lazarus would have been the talk of the town and surrounding areas for months, years even. And wasn't it written down in the Gospels of Matthew, Mark, and Luke? Was it that they were not impressed? And why did no one ask Lazarus about what it was like after he died? Wouldn't that be the first question that people would ask him?"

"I hear you, bro. Me being the way I am, *I* would have bombarded him with questions. I still want to ask you about how life continues before we run out of time here on earth."

I figured he had said all he wanted to say about the Bible, but I had one more question about the Gospels.

"Just one more question, Josh, and we can move on. Why is John's Gospel so different from the first three Gospels?"

"Yes, John's Gospel is strikingly different in what it teaches than what we read in the first three. The author of the Gospel of John writes about being 'born again,' and that I was, in fact, God. His pervasive theme is that I was the only way to get to heaven. The first three Gospels paint quite a different picture, which was, 'Try to live as Jesus lived if you want a happy, peaceful, fulfilled life.'"

"So who's telling the truth?" I asked.

"Well, there are *elements* of truth in all four Gospels, but all contain things that the early Christians interpreted and added rather than accurately reporting what I really said—and did. It's just the way things were done at that time in history. You had a message you wanted to get out, but sometimes you had to exaggerate and put words into people's mouths in order to gain followers, no matter what the message was that was being promoted. The author of the Gospel of John wasn't interested in writing history or science or what have you. He had a theological agenda: to persuade as many people as possible to 'believe' in me."

"Believe *what* about you?" I interjected.

"To believe that I was God in human form who was sent by God to die on the cross for the sins of humanity. That is the essence of Paul's religion. Paul never talked about my life and teaching. In fact, Paul knew almost nothing about me. But what Paul wrote in his letters has been the official Christian party line ever since Christianity was made the only recognized official religion by Emperor Constantine in the early fourth century."

Joshua was standing up now, walking around the living room in ever-widening circles.

"The Bible itself does not claim that everything in it is historically true or scientifically accurate. That's something that Jews and then Christians believed and was the view that came out on top after centuries of religious debate and political maneuvering. But you won't find that view in the Bible itself. Look at it this way: none of the authors of the Bible had any idea that their books and letters and stories and poetry would be eventually collected and canonized into one book—the 'infallible word of God.' It pays to keep in mind, too, that sacred scriptures in every faith tradition claim to be 'straight from the mouth of God.' So it's a circular argument that doesn't make sense."

"Yeah, I hear you. It's like, it seems to me that most Christians live in a kind of impenetrable bubble that you just can't break through. Anyone who questions the basic beliefs is just ignored as being 'liberal' who doesn't 'know the Lord.' For evangelical and Catholic Christians, the Bible is the final authority on all matters of life and faith."

"Granted, but there is a tremendous security inside the bubble. They don't claim to merely believe that their faith is true—they're *certain* of it. And certainty about anything basically stops all dialogue and discussion. What I'm telling you now is something that most Christians aren't aware of. In ancient traditions, those preceding the writing of the Bible, their scriptures all record stories about the creation of humans, the flood, how different ethnicities and languages came about, and on and on. My point is that the writers of the Bible did a lot of 'borrowing' from more ancient sources, including the whole God coming to earth in human form and dying and rising from the dead to save people from their sins."

"So you're saying that the stories in the Bible, including what you are recorded as saying and doing, can be found in other ancient traditions that predate the Bible?"

"Yes. It goes along with the times. Every culture since the beginning of human time developed beliefs about the nature of God and the visible universe. And those shared beliefs captured basic morality as societies evolved—ways of thinking and doing things that would ensure their survival and well-being: don't steal from others, respect the property of others, do not lie, cheat, or kill. Eventually these moralities became codified into what we now call 'religion.' The point is this: there's nothing in the Bible that can't be found in earlier ancient religions."

"So is there anything unique in the Bible, things that you don't find in other ancient religions?"

"No. It's all been said before. Every religion has their sacred scriptures that their adherents believe came straight from the mouth of God. And they're all wrong. I was chosen by God to tell the truth and make it clear to people who God is." He winked at me with that wry smile of his and continued, "Referring back to the four Gospel accounts of my life by Matthew, Mark, Luke, and John, I can tell you straight up that these were collections of my life and teachings, but mostly quite sketchy and, in some places, downright *confusing*—including stuff the writers just made up. The first record of these accounts of my life with the authors' names attached to them didn't appear until after the Jewish revolt against the Romans in AD 70, which resulted in the destruction of the Jewish temple and much of Jerusalem, many years after my life, death, and resurrection. Plus, Rog, did you know that there are actually over twenty other Gospels that purport to contain my life and teachings?"

"Well, you told me about Mary Magdalene's Gospel. So why were these other Gospels not included in the Bible?" I asked.

"These twenty or so other Gospels were deemed by the religious elite at the time not to support what the Apostle Paul wrote, so they were branded as 'heresies' and burned or destroyed whenever they came across a copy. It's such a shame, because many of my real teachings and parables are much more true and accurate in those Gospels than in the four Gospels that you currently have in your Bible. Take the Gospel of Thomas, for example. Thomas's Gospel was written about the same time as Matthew and Luke but was deemed to be heretical because it contained some of my teachings that were considered not to be in accord with those Gospels and Paul's letters. Copies of the Gospel of Thomas were then hidden by the Thomas Christians so they wouldn't be destroyed. The Gospel of John, by the way, was written about a decade after the Gospel of Thomas started being circulating around the various Christian communities."

"When did we find out about the other Gospels, like the Gospel of Thomas?" I asked.

"Many secret Gospels and writings were discovered just last century, at Nag Hamadi in Egypt. Have you heard of the Dead Sea Scrolls?"

"I have, Josh. I just didn't know what, exactly, was found there. So what is it about the Gospel of Thomas that so pissed off the author of the Gospel of John?" I asked.

"The Gospel of Thomas is not an account of my life, but it consists of one hundred and fourteen teachings, parables, and aphorisms that I learned in my travels before coming back to Palestine in my late twenties. I had thought about what I learned in India and elsewhere for a long time, and I decided to take these timeless truths and make them clear and applicable to the lives of my followers. Sometimes it didn't go so well; they could be very thickheaded at times, but I think they caught on to the important stuff. But Mary Magdalene got *all* of it. I was so proud of her!"

I could almost *feel* how he felt about her.

He continued, "My point in telling you all this is that no human being really knows how the four Gospels now found in the Bible were written and compiled and how the names of the four alleged authors got attached to their respective books. The most glaring example of this is that Matthew, Mark, and Luke really didn't know anything about the real *implications* of my life and teaching. But John's Gospel does contain a fairly well developed theology. And why? As I said earlier, John's Gospel wasn't written until two generations after my death. The author was an old man when he wrote this Gospel, and he wasn't one of my disciples as many Christians think. Anyway, you can't have it both ways. I could go on and on about how there are obvious later additions and made-up stuff in all four Gospels, material that some religious leaders decades after my life and death thought it best to add in order to further their own agenda of power and control. It really is all about *control*. To Christians today, though, what I'm telling you undermines the whole sense that the Gospels and the Bible as a whole are free from error and contradictions, thus undermining the belief in the Bible's reliability."

He paused, so I jumped in.

"Okay, Josh, I'm with you, I think. But if the Bible is not reliable, then how do we know what's true and what isn't when we read it?" I asked.

"The same way you know *anything*—by using your *reason*. The human brain has evolved into something akin to a supercomputer. We use our minds many times every day to determine what is fact and what is fiction and what falls in between. So here's the deal: The current version of the Bible, as we know it, sometimes *contains* truth and tells us about God, as do the sacred scriptures of every religious tradition, but it's up to *you* to figure out what is fact and what is fiction and what truth is being communicated. Know what I mean?"

"I do, my man, but doesn't that lead to all sorts of disagreements and bad feelings among Christians?" I asked.

"Welcome to the real world. Yeah, it does. It is what it is." He quickly stood up and, using his best Neil deGrasse Tyson voice, said loudly, "Climate change is real!"

"Okay," I said, not all that impressed. "So we have to figure out for ourselves what's true and what isn't in the Bible. Won't that rock the Christian world? Especially hearing it from *you*?" I asked.

"I don't know, but it's been going on for centuries, often times creating a climate of violence and hatred. Is that what I was all about?" he asked.

"No," I responded. But there was something that I *had* to ask him about the God portrayed in the Bible before we moved on.

Chapter Forty-Two

Joshua excused himself to go to the washroom. I turned to Joseph and asked, "Have you heard all this before, Joe?"

"Most of it, yes, but hearing it from the Lord today makes me think of all the bad stuff that has accompanied religion through the centuries. We angels have had the ability and privilege to follow human history, and we're troubled by what has gone on. You guys—humans, that is—are extremely difficult for us angels to understand."

"But don't you think it's easier for angels to live lives pleasing to God? I mean, you know about spiritual realities and God's agenda. Us humans don't. Can you imagine what that's like for us?"

"Kind of, I guess. But meeting you, Rog, and hanging out both in the psych ward and now here in your apartment has given me a real appreciation for what it must be like to be human and to have to live life here on earth. I consider myself very fortunate to have been given this opportunity."

"Me too, Joe. I'm learning so much today that is challenging my thinking about spiritual reality. I mean, here I am, a *human,* hanging out with Jesus Christ and an angel! How fortunate is *that?*"

"I'm learning too, Rog. It's rare that an angel gets to hang out with the Lord."

We looked at each other with tears in our eyes. Instinctively we both rose out of our chairs at the same time and embraced.

I looked into his face and asked, "Joe, is this what you look like in the heavenly realm? I mean, what's the deal with having no teeth?"

Joseph chuckled at that. "No, and someday you'll see me in my realm. I'm quite the stud if I do say so myself. But angels can take on different appearances when required, and this is what I wanted to look like for this assignment. I guess that's why I like drinking beer. It's difficult to eat solid food with no teeth."

"Okay, let's grab a couple. I'll get one for Joshua too."

Chapter Forty-Three

Joshua returned from the washroom, sat down at the kitchen table, and grabbed his beer. We sat there in silence for a moment, drinking.

"I was thinking of something while I was away that I think you should know. I was a man of my times. I tried hard to be a good Jew and follow all the social rules and dietary regulations. God chose me to proclaim the Kingdom of God message that was meant for all human beings."

I was a bit stunned when Joseph said, "Lord, things are certainly different for you ever since God chose you to be his son at your baptism so many years ago. My question is: Do you know everything about the universe now? Have you explored the universe to its very boundaries?"

"No, Joe. Only God knows the full extent of his creation. When I lived here back in the day, I believed, along with everyone else, that the earth was the center of the universe. The prevailing truth was that the sun rotated around the earth and that the earth was flat. I believed all that. I even contributed to the confusion about God's reality. I believed, along with everyone else, that God was up in the sky somewhere. I taught my followers to pray to God 'who lives in heaven.' I was wrong about that and lots of other things. True, I know a lot more about the universe and God's reality than most, but I'm still learning. I'll tell you this, though: earth is not special, nor is it the center of the universe. Here's how to think about the size of the universe: think of picking up one grain of sand next time you go to the beach. One grain. That is the size of the earth in relation to *all* the sand in the world—on land, under water, everywhere. Can you grasp that, Rog?"

I couldn't.

He winked at Joseph and continued, "And that's just a raw comparison. I can tell you, too, that the universe continues to expand, even while we're sitting here talking."

"Okay, Josh, I get that it's a big universe—"

"But back to what we were talking about, I just want to say one more thing about the accounts of my life as found in the Gospels. By the middle of the second century, there were over twenty other written Gospels that were in circulation among the various Christian communities. These other Gospels were deemed by those who were following Paul's religion to be fakes because they didn't line up with what Paul wrote in his letters, so they were branded as 'heresies' and burned or destroyed. Many of my actual teachings and things that I did are much more accurate in some of those Gospels than in the four Gospels that you currently have in your Bible."

"Can you give me an example of what you're talking about?" I asked.

"Yeah. Remember that Thomas's Gospel was written about the same time as Matthew and Luke were written, but it was deemed to be heretical because it contained some of my teachings that were considered not to be in accord with those Gospels and Paul's letters. Copies of the Gospel of Thomas began to be circulated and later hidden by the Thomas Christians so they wouldn't be destroyed. The Gospel of John was written about a decade after the Gospel of Thomas with the intent of undermining it. That was one of the main reasons the author of the Gospel of John wrote what he did. Thomas faithfully captured my words that the Kingdom of God is *within* you. The author of John didn't agree with that, so he made Thomas out to be a coward."

"When did we find out about some of these other Gospels?" I asked.

"As I said a minute ago, dude, many of these other Gospels and writings were discovered just last century, in Egypt and Israel, right after the end of World War II—commonly known as the Dead Sea Scrolls. The Gospel of Thomas was discovered about fifty years before that even. And there will be other discoveries of other writings from the first century in the near future."

Man, I was amazed at what he was telling me. I wondered about what other Gospels or writings might be discovered in future years.

Joshua continued, "But remember, Mary was the only one to really get it."

"Oh, man," I thought. "I have to get him to talk more about . . ."

So I did.

Chapter Forty-Four

I said a bit tentatively, "So you really loved that woman, it sounds like."

"Man, Rog, I loved her to death and sure wish I could have married her and have kids with her. But I was *so* busy and *so* focused on what my Dad had sent me here to do; it simply was not possible."

"I admire that, Josh," I said. Then I thought, "But why?" I wasn't sure.

"We usually hung out together while we were walking from one place to another, and we tried to be alone together whenever we could. We would kiss passionately a lot when we could find some privacy. She had the most beautiful mouth and pouty lips that just drove me crazy when we would kiss. But Mary and I weren't just physically intimate; I shared my deepest thoughts and emotions with her too. She really was my muse. I would tell her things that I never told my disciples, even to this day. We were emotionally intimate."

I just looked at him with my eyes wide open and my jaw dropping almost to the kitchen table.

He didn't miss a beat. "Mary even wrote her own Gospel, her own account of our experiences together. Did you know that?" he asked.

I was trying to get my mouth working again so that I could form actual words.

"No," I finally managed. "So why isn't it well known that your woman wrote her own story about you? I'm kind of stunned about that. Can you tell me more about it?" I asked.

"Well," he said, "it was relatively short, not like the long, drawn-out Gospels written by the men. She lets my disciples in on the not-so-secret fact that we were emotionally intimate and that I had told her things that I hadn't told them. They were not excited to hear that. Not excited at all."

"Can you tell me more about it and some of the things she kept secret?" I asked.

"A little bit," he said. "If I told you everything, then they wouldn't be secrets. I will say, though, that my disciples were quite disgusted with her. She wrote about that too. At one point she wrote about how Peter, as leader of the disciples, asked her to tell them some of the secrets that I had told her. This was after my Dad raised me from the dead. Peter said something along the lines of, 'You need to tell us the secrets he told you so that we can know them too.'

"Her response was similar to what I just mentioned a moment ago: 'If I told you the secrets he told me, then they wouldn't be secrets, would they?' Peter and the rest of the guys were incensed.

"According to Mary, Peter said, 'We know that the Lord loved you more than the rest of us, but you're still just a *woman*.'"

I was stunned by what he was telling me. Why hadn't I heard about this before? Why wasn't it widespread news that Mary Magdalene had written about him? This was almost too much for me to comprehend.

"I know what you mean, Rog. My Dad and I aren't happy about how the early church leaders, all men of course, did their best not to let anyone know about what Mary had written. It's a travesty and one of the reasons I'm sitting here talking with you today. It's wrong, and I want everyone who will listen to know it's wrong."

I was transfixed. I didn't really know what I expected him to say during this interview, but I knew I hadn't expected *this*. I couldn't help but ask, "So can you tell me *some* of the things you told her that you didn't tell your disciples?"

He sat silent for a moment. His eyes were closed, and his head was down.

"Yeah, I will, Rog. This is what I came here to do. One time she asked me about 'sin'; what it is, and what we're supposed to do about it. I told her the truth that I learned from my Father. I told her, 'There is no sin. Human beings *create* sin when they do what they know is wrong.' Then I told her, 'Matter gives birth to a passion that has no equal, which proceeds from something contrary to the natural order—contrary to nature itself.'"

My jaw was hanging down to my belly button. The only word I could crank out was, "*What?*"

"That's okay," he said. "That's why I was a bit hesitant to share with you what I taught her. But that's why I'm here, so I'll just tell you stuff, the consequences be damned. I'm so sick and tired of all the bullshit coming from my so-called followers today."

"Thank you, Joshua. Don't worry about me understanding everything. I think the important thing is that the readers of this interview will at least *know* that you shared secrets with Mary that you didn't share with your other disciples."

He sat there silently.

"Don't let me get in the way, Josh. Say what you came here to say," I said.

"I will, Rog," he said. "In Mary's Gospel, she relates that one time Peter came to her and said, 'We know that the Lord loves you more than he does us. That's not right. He didn't call you, a woman, to be one of the twelve disciples; he called *us*, us *men*, to be his disciples. So get back in your place and keep your mouth shut. You're a woman, for God's sake!'"

I was listening intently.

He continued, "But here's the deal, Rog. The disciples were not ignorant about what was going on with me and Mary. We were in love. We tried to be discreet, but it was pretty difficult to be discreet in small towns and in our travels from village to village. Sometimes we just had to 'spirit away' so that we could spend some time alone together."

"*Hmmm . . .*," I thought, "I wonder what he means by 'spirit away'?"

He evidently ignored my thought, because he picked up where he left off.

"And remember that the plan is for this memoir to receive worldwide attention, so please be careful not to change a word of what I'm telling you."

"I get it, Josh. I will stay faithful to what you're telling me when this ends up in book form," I promised.

"I felt that I could tell Mary anything and trust her with my innermost thoughts. I told her about how the universe is teeming with life on millions and millions of planets. I taught her how to go deep inside for spiritual insights by focusing on her inner self. I taught her how to disappear and reappear somewhere else far away, something I never taught my disciples. She was constantly by my side, much to the embarrassment and outrage of the twelve. My male disciples constantly harangued me about how bad it looked to people that I had a close female companion. But I didn't care. I loved her more than anyone else on earth. In the end, though, as you now know, they buried her testimony from the public record—and virtually buried her memory as well."

Omigod! I was dumbfounded. I know I keep saying how awestruck I was by what he was telling me in this interview, but perhaps my repetition underscores how I was feeling.

"Josh, can you give me a hint as to some specific things you taught her?" I asked excitedly.

"I can," he said. "There's a hint of what I tried to get across to all my followers in Matthew's Gospel. Not much of what I really taught made it into the four Gospels; most of what is recorded are words that were put into my mouth to further a religious and political agenda. But this one I did teach. I said to my disciples many times, 'If your eye be single, your whole body will be full of light.' I learned this in my travels in India before I began my public ministry. I tried to explain that to my followers in many different ways, but they just couldn't grasp it. Remember that my disciples were a mixture of illiterate fishermen, farmers, and blue-collar types. I tried and tried, and finally I realized that only one was catching on to what I was teaching—that one being Mary Magdalene. She was sharp as a whip."

"And?" I asked.

"How people live, that is, what they believe, and how what they believe influences the way they live and act in this life is based on a number of things, but the most influential one is what they are taught from childhood to *believe*, or what they decide later in life to believe. Belief and faith are the strongest determinants of how people live their lives. If you use your intuition and look deep within yourself, your mind will be free, and with that freedom comes illumination. That's why I kept teaching people that the Kingdom of God is *within* you. It's not rocket science, Rog—as I said many times in my public teaching, 'The Truth is within you. Search within yourself and you will find it.'"

I was starting to squirm. I didn't get it. So I asked him, "Truth about *what*?"

He looked at me with a smile and said, "The Truth about what is *real*, about reality—about *God's* reality. That's why I'm here—to set the record straight about God's reality, his Dream, and how human beings can actually understand God's reality."

He paused for moment to see if that would sink in. It didn't. He knew it too.

He sighed and said, "What I taught Mary Magdalene was that any human being can experience a continual *peace* in his or her life, and joy, happiness, and freedom, *despite* one's individual circumstances or upbringing. When one chooses to know the Truth, one's life is changed from the inside. What human beings have called 'heaven' or 'paradise' is available to you *right now*. As I told my followers, you can bring God's reality to *earth* as it is in heaven. Merely turn inward, and your eye will be single, and your whole body will be full of light."

"Okay, Joshua," I said in quiet desperation. "I'm not really sure what you mean yet, but I feel as if I now at least have a clue."

"Good for you, Rog. Everything truly can be 'on earth as it is in heaven.' Mary understood this, and she was able to cross dimensions here on earth."

"Really?" I thought. "Cross dimensions?"

"Yes," he replied to my thoughts. "Until your eye is single and you realize that everything is of God, your life will be one of discord, illusion, and heartache."

Chapter Forty-Five

I asked, "Earlier you used the phrase 'God's reality.' Can you give me some examples of what you mean by God's reality?"

"Let me do that by telling you what God's reality is *not*," he replied. "God's reality is not about punishment or condemnation or judgment. It is *not* about him being angry when human beings screw up their lives, or even the lives of others. His love for you is unconditional. You have to think about that. There is no 'if' in *his mind*. After this earth experience, everyone will see that he loves all his creation without condition. You don't have to 'do this' or 'do that' or 'believe this' or 'believe that' to somehow *earn* God's love and acceptance. I'll say it again: God doesn't *need* anything. Life continues after this one, and you *are* accepted and loved by God no matter how you live your life or what you believe. When you learn to allow your eye to be single, you will understand these things. You can begin to let your eye be single by putting aside everything you think you know about God and religion and your sense of reality. Then you will experience how what *you do not* believe will transform your life and relationships.

"My point in telling you all this is that the story of how the four Gospels now found in the Bible were agreed upon relates to which version of Christianity gained the most converts over the first three centuries after my death. After the Roman Emperor Constantine decided for political purposes to declare Christianity the official state religion of the Roman Empire in the early fourth century, the version of Christianity that had gained the most converts was Paul's. So the followers of Paul, like the vast majority of Christians since then, became the official decision-makers about such things as who I was, what my death meant, what books should be included in the Bible, the concept of the Trinity, and so on."

"Okay, so how do we know what you actually said and did if we have to sift through all these manuscripts that are unreliable?"

"By relying on biblical scholars, historians, and textual critics; people who have dedicated their entire careers to learning the ancient languages and applying their knowledge and skills to determine what *probably* happened and what I *probably* taught and did. Then you have to determine which scholars *you* trust the same way you know *anything*—by using your minds, your *reason*. The Bible sometimes *contains* truth about God and reality, just like any other book, but it's up to you to figure out what is fact and what is fiction and what truth is being communicated."

"But doesn't that lead to all sorts of disagreements and bad feelings among Christians?" I asked.

"Yeah, it does. That's why there are over five thousand different Christian denominations today, all claiming to be the only 'true' representation of what I taught. I'm hoping this interview will shake the foundations of the Christian churches around the world. My hope is that people will begin to come to an awareness of who God really is and how we evolved as a human species and finally begin to abandon religion altogether."

"*Hmmm . . . ,*" I thought, "I can't really see *that* happening."

"Neither can I, dude, but you gotta try, right?"

Chapter Forty-Six

I said, "Okay, I want you to clear up something once and for all. The God you revealed back in the day was a compassionate, loving, and forgiving God. But in the Old Testament of the Bible what we see is a God, who is frequently petty, angry, vicious, misogynistic, homophobic . . ."

"Okay, Rog, I get where you're going with this. I guess I'm just a bit surprised is all about how strongly you feel about how the Old Testament portrays God."

"More than just a strong feeling, Josh. When I decided to go to Bible college, the whole image of God as seen in the Old Testament *haunted* me. That and the problem of needless pain and suffering in the world are the main things keeping me from *totally* trusting God. And now here I am talking with you, and I really, really want to know the *truth* about this."

Joshua closed his eyes and put his forehead down on the table on his arms. After a moment he raised his head and looked straight at me.

"You're right, Rog. That is something I need to clear up while I'm here. Those who believe that the Bible is literally the infallible 'Word of God' have always had a big problem with how God is portrayed in the Old Testament.

"Let me try and set the stage for what I'm about to tell you. Over the centuries Jews and Christians have read and listened to what I would call the 'good parts' of the Bible. In the Old Testament, for example, most people have heard about the cool stories: Adam and Eve, Cain and Abel, Noah and the Ark, the

Tower of Babel—that kind of stuff. As the Bible tells it, God wanted his 'chosen people' to live 'good' lives and to eventually inhabit the 'promised land.' But very, very few Christians have taken the time to actually *read* the Old Testament, much less study it and try to make sense of it. The problem is that millions of people over the centuries actually believe that the Old Testament gives a true picture of who God is and how God relates to human beings. As we talked about earlier, the God of the universe had nothing to do with the writing of the Old Testament."

"Look, the Old Testament gets off to a confusing start right from the beginning of Genesis. Everyone knows the first three words of Genesis: 'In the beginning.' But almost immediately the book begins to fall apart. You'd think that God would have his shit together right at the start and pretty much know where he's going with the whole creation thing. But he doesn't. He seems to get confused right from the start. The first two days, he creates big stuff: light, sky, water, and earth, but then the third day is devoted to making plants. Then he gets back to the big stuff on the fourth day by creating the sun, moon, and stars. And then God decides to scatter human beings around the world and tells them to 'Enjoy the gift of Life! Get to it! Fill the earth with your kind!' Nothing is said about how human beings have evolved over millions of years. But the one thing that you human types have been *very* good at is reproducing, and it doesn't take a genius to figure out why. Can you imagine how the first humans figured *that* out? And having found out *how*, well, the rest is history."

Now we all three were laughing together, and it felt so *good*! Here I was in the privileged position of hanging out with Jesus Christ as if he was my BFF, along with an angel of the Lord who really *was* becoming my BFF. I was on cloud nine! How I wish people could see a video of Joshua, Joseph, and me talking together and taking side trips back in time. What effect would *that* have on Christians today?

Joshua picked up where he had left off. "Well, one of what many Jews and Christians agree is one of the coolest stories in the Bible is the story of Noah and the Ark. But when you actually *read* the story, you begin to wonder about this God of theirs. First, the Bible tells us, God is extremely pissed off at all the evil and killing that humans were doing to each other. Their sins are never specified, but God must have thought they were hopelessly degenerate. He expresses regret that he had ever created humans in the first place. He says, 'I wish I had never made these evil creatures.' So he decides what he's going to do is—wait for it!—*kill them*! Kill them all and start all over again."

"Which he does, if I remember correctly," I said.

"True, although, according to the story, there was *one guy* who God still liked: Noah. So God decided to save Noah and his family from being killed in the flood that God was to use as his weapon of choice for killing all other human beings on the earth at that time. God told them to build a big boat, load tons of animals on it, and be saved from the flood. The rest, as they say, is history. Except for one thing: it's not; it's just a story. It tells about a god who is quick to anger and swift in his punishment—a very dark god, to be sure.

"We read further in Genesis of the treachery and deceitfulness of God's chosen people. All the stories that follow are full of deception, rape, treachery, human trafficking, and lots and lots of killing. And the God of the Old Testament loves it! He commands them to do it, and then he blesses them."

"I don't think many Sunday school lessons would include—"

"No, they don't. How could they? And those are just a few stories from the first book of the Old Testament," Joshua said quietly. "As you already know, it gets worse. *Much* worse."

"Well, I think people today need to know what's really in the Old Testament, especially Christians who take the Bible seriously," I said.

"All we need to do is look at some things that the God of the Old Testament commanded his 'chosen people' to do. In the books of Leviticus and Deuteronomy, we find the following:

Anyone found out to be homosexual must be killed.

Any child who rebels against his parents must be killed.

Anyone who is caught working on the Sabbath must be killed.

If an ox gores someone, both the ox and the man who owned the ox must be put to death.

("Why the ox?" I wondered.)

Any woman who has sex outside of marriage must be killed.

If a girl is being raped and doesn't yell loud enough, she must be killed.

"Yikes!" I blurted out. "I . . . I don't know what to say. I've heard of some shady dealings by God in the Old Testament, but this stuff?" I was beyond further speech.

"And that's just what the God of the Old Testament commands his 'chosen people' to do. It gets worse. Here are a few things that God himself will do to *anyone* who doesn't worship him:

God punishes the children for the sins of their parents if they worship other gods.

God will kill children and unborn fetuses if their parents worship other gods.

God will make men's wives into whores and their daughters into sex slaves if they worship other gods.

God will kill righteous men and forget their good deeds if they turn to sin.

"I could go on and on, Rog, but I think it best we stop here. What I've given you is but a small sample of how the Old Testament portrays God."

I was done.

"I'm telling you as clearly as I can, Rog. *That's not who God is*. The portrayal of God in the Old Testament was a Bronze Age conception of a god that all Jews had grown up with. He's just not like that. The whole portrayal of God in the Old Testament is fatally flawed."

"Thank God!" I said sincerely.

Chapter Forty-Seven

I shuffled my notes with my questions on them and tried to settle down and compose myself. "I kind of want to go back a bit by asking you this, Josh: Why did God appoint you to be his son? Like, why *you*?"

"God knew that no religion portrayed him as he really is. He decided to adopt me as his son and messenger to show all people *who he really is* and how much love and compassion he has for all human beings. But he had to do it in time, in history, just as he has appointed many, many messengers and 'sons and daughters' over the millennium. I'm not unique in that respect, although for various historical and cultural reasons, I guess you could say I am one of the most well-known figures in human history. I was the first child born at that exact time in history to come from King David's lineage, so it made sense that I would be anointed as the Jewish Messiah and chosen to be God's 'son.' My reason for being here now is exactly the same as it was back in the day: to tell people about God's love for them and to encourage people to trust in God for all their needs and to treat others as they would like to be treated."

"Okay, okay," I said. "I do believe I'm starting to get it, Josh. Now I see why you never taught about what happens after a person dies. That will take care of itself. Now I get it that all we really need to do is to try to live life to the fullest every day of our lives and be focused on others if we want to be happy in this life. I guess I've always been hung up on what happens to us after we die, so I didn't really *get* it that you were talking about this present life on earth when you taught about the Kingdom of God."

"That's right, Rog. Life continues after this one. That's a given. My final teaching to my followers, and by extension to all human beings, was to *love one another* and to be *united* in God's love. That hasn't happened yet."

He raised his eyes to mine. I could see that he was getting very emotional about this.

"Most of what the Christian Church has taught about me over the past two thousand years is just plain wrong. And that has hurt literally millions of people throughout the centuries, people who really wanted to put their trust in God but were so turned off by the violence and bloodshed and hatred that has been perpetrated in my name, *Jesus Christ*: the Crusades and the Inquisition, wars, racism, slavery, killing people for thought crimes or for not believing the 'right way,' intolerance, ethnocide; the list goes on and on. What a person believes strongly influences that person's behavior." After a brief pause, he said, "Going hand in hand with that is that very few Christians are able to explain *why* they believe *what* they believe, be it the concept that God is actually three different personalities or the teaching that *I* am God, much less be able to explain such concepts without sounding like they're cuckoo for coco puffs. Both of those beliefs took a long time to take hold; it took centuries for such beliefs to become codified as official Church teachings."

He looked intently at me to see if I was focusing. I was.

"And think, too, of what kinds of views these religious leaders, who were exclusively men, had about the world around them: the inferiority of women, homosexuality, infanticide, extreme nationalism, and so on. No one believes the world is flat anymore. Yet primitive thinking continues to rear its ugly head even today in every religion. Being gay is still seen as a sinful lifestyle choice. Women are still considered inferior to men. Racism is rampant in the religious world. Intolerance is the norm. And worst of all, Christians, following the religion of Paul of Tarsus are thought to be following the one true path to God because they continue to believe that the Bible is the infallible 'Word of God.' Again, that, in essence, is why I'm here with you today. I'm here to set the record straight about God's reality."

Joshua's face looked strained. He was obviously agitated, frustrated, and upset by his last words.

I tried to calm him down by letting him know that I had his back on this. I understood why he was upset and why he was here today doing this interview.

"I'm with you, my friend. I get it. What you're doing here today is going to change the world."

"That remains to be seen, Rog, but I think my disappointment about the past and current state of Christianity is because of one man: Paul of Tarsus. Paul came up with his own religion, which gained widespread acceptance because of a variety of political, philosophical, and yes, *religious* reasons. By the time Christianity became the official religion of the Roman Empire in the fourth century, the die was cast. Paul's religion won out over a number of differing Christian movements. The Kingdom of God message that God chose me to proclaim to the world was dead. I'm here to change that."

"You will, Josh—I can *feel* it. This will become a momentous day in human history."

"I so hope you're right, Rog. Christians have been spreading a false message that no one can 'get to heaven' except by becoming a Christian, and only the 'right kind' of Christian. Most Christians today believe that Christianity is the only path by which a person is able to enter the Kingdom of God."

I'd heard *that* before. Many times.

"Most Christians today and throughout the centuries believe that I came to save them from their sins. That's not the message I proclaimed. My teaching about God's Kingdom was always in tandem with a call for people to change their hearts and minds about how you live and relate to God and others. The problem that human beings face is not with what you guys call 'sin' but with *fear*. I was constantly telling my followers to have *faith*. The central human problem is with *fear*—fear of dying, fear of living, fear of spiders, or whatever."

That struck home. "Yeah," I said, "fear can dominate our lives—*my* life. Mostly fear of the unknown: what's going to happen to me here on earth, and what's going to happen after I die."

"That's why I taught that the important things in life boil down to learning to trust God for *everything*—living without fear or anxiety and being concerned for the well-being of others. This whole thing about being afraid of death or whatever is a barrier to living life to the fullest in the here and now. Why are people afraid of death? I provided everyone with the greatest example of why fear or anxiety should not be a part of one's life. I lived out the values of God's Kingdom, God's Dream, in my daily life, was crucified, and died. Then God raised me from the dead. I was seen and heard by dozens of people, including my followers. And what did I tell them? 'See? God raised me up from the dead *just as he will raise you up after you die*!' You don't need to stress about what happens to you after you die. Life continues. Focus all your energies instead on living life to the fullest while here on earth, helping others and showing love and compassion to all."

Joshua was passionate about this, and I was feeling that passion.

"My mission was to *liberate* people from their fears and anxieties and to encourage all people to learn to live happy, meaningful lives by trusting God to always provide whatever one needs and to be compassionate toward others. Like, it's up to you. Trust God, and you can have a cool, meaningful life, or trust in yourself and live a life filled with fear, anxiety, and well, a crummy life always waiting for the other shoe to drop. My own sense of trust in life comes from my intimate relationship with God, which he wants to have with every person."

"I think I need a drink," I said.

"I wouldn't mind one myself."

Chapter Forty-Eight

I took a quick glance at the clock on the wall, but Joshua was way ahead of me.

"Yeah, maybe time for a break anyway," he said.

It was 7:15 p.m., and I was feeling pretty exhausted—hungry too. Interviewing Jesus was no easy task. Plus I kept fretting about how we were going to get through all my questions with the time we had left—just so much ground to cover.

"We'll be okay," Joshua said quietly. "I'm getting pretty hungry myself. What about you, Joseph?"

I hadn't noticed that Joseph had gotten up during the interview session. "Maybe he had to use the bathroom," I thought. "I'll have to remember to ask him if he even needs to go to the bathroom."

Suddenly Joseph just seemed to suddenly appear in the living room.

I wondered to myself if angels, too, could appear and reappear at will.

"Yes, they can, although it's much more difficult to do things like that while on earth. The atmosphere is just so heavy. Angels are pretty fascinated with human beings. You guys are quite the enigma to angels."

He glanced over at Joseph, who was now sitting on the couch.

"Right, Joe?"

"You're always right, Lord. I've been learning so much more about you and humans by being able to sit in with you guys."

Joshua stood up and said, "Well, maybe we should get back to our dinner plans."

I felt a bit embarrassed. "As you guys know, I'm stretched pretty thin these days financially. Do either of you happen to have any money? Or maybe a credit card?"

Joshua answered, "I've got this. Let's order a big, fully loaded pizza! No anchovies, though. Can you make the arrangements?"

"Sure." So I did.

We were waiting for the delivery guy when Joshua asked *me* a question.

"So, Rog, do you have any guilt or anxiety or fear of dying? Do you feel like you're living life to the fullest every day?"

"Well, no to everything, to be honest," I said. "But meeting you, and Joseph, too, is really making me reflect on my life. I mean, I like to think I'm a nice guy: a good partner to Sylvie, and a loving, caring father, a good friend, willing to help others out when I can—you know, that kind of stuff."

Joshua chuckled. "Yeah, you *are* a good guy, Rog. *I* like you, anyway. So how is hanging out with me and Joe going to impact how you live your life?"

"*Hmmm . . .*" I was at a loss for words. But, being me, I came up with some anyway. "Well, you *are* Jesus, and I'm actually spending time with you and an angel, so like, yeah, I feel that I'm reflecting on my life through this experience and that it is changing me—*going* to change me."

Joshua and Joseph glanced at each other, smiling.

"Can I ask you guys a question?"

"Sure," Joseph answered. "What's on your mind?"

"I know the outcome is assured and that all human beings will continue living after this life on earth, but can you guys tell me what that will be like? I mean, don't you get asked that question a lot in your . . . travels or whatever?"

Kind of weak, I thought, but I was serious.

Joshua checked in, "Well, what you guys call 'heaven' is a feeble attempt to capture spiritual reality in words. It just can't be described in a way that makes sense to people in the twenty-first century. Maybe it did the trick back in the day, but today it just sounds like a fairy tale. You really think that God actually sits on a big throne somewhere?"

"Well, no, but I like to think that he's *somewhere.*"

"Okay, Rog, fair enough. Listen carefully, although very few are likely to believe you when you tell them what I'm about to tell you."

He paused as if to carefully consider what he wanted to tell me.

"What human beings refer to as 'heaven,' or 'paradise,' or 'nirvana,' or whatever, well, your life after this earthly one is inconceivable to the human mind. For thousands of years, even into the twenty-first century, the vast majority of religious people have believed that 'heaven' is a place. It's not. It's a continuation of your life, your personality in a different kind of body; you'll know who you are, and you'll remember your time on earth. But it won't all be peaches and cream. No religion or philosophy has ever really thought about this. What humans think of as 'heaven' is not all that it's cracked up to be."

"You're kind of making me nervous, Josh," I said. "I get it that life continues, but doesn't that imply that everything is, I don't know, perfect and exciting, right?" I wasn't sure how else to say it.

"No, not right, Rog. What I'm telling you now is difficult for humans to grasp, but it's the truth. It's a physical universe, and all human beings will continue living in that universe. As life continues after this one, it will still have its challenges and difficulties, its highs and lows, its cool stuff and its hardships. It's difficult to even use language to try to describe it to you. I'll give you a few examples, though. First, most people throughout human history have believed that they'll 'know everything' after they die and go to 'heaven.'"

"Won't we, Josh? I thought you said that it was a given."

"No, you'll know that life continues and that God exists, but you enter the next stage of life with your own personal stock of knowledge, skill sets, deficiencies, and so on. You will be who you are. But learning continues, if you want to keep learning, and you'll experience all sorts of things that you experience and deal with here on earth. Do you have people here on earth whom you have a problem with? Don't think that everything will be fine and dandy in the next life. It won't. Will you be willing to try and reconcile with those people? Or what about your prejudices and racism and homophobia or *whatever*. Do you think they will magically disappear from your mind in the next life? Why do you believe that? Life does continue, but it is based on the same realities you experience here on earth: relationships, learning new things, maturing in thought, growing in knowledge, treating others the way you want to be treated, or not, always in a process of *becoming*, but you'll still have choices to make; you will still and always will have *free will*."

I didn't know what to say or even think about what he was telling me. So I blurted out, "Okay, Josh, maybe other people will understand what you're talking about, but can you bring it down a notch for me?"

"Sure, Rog. The hope is that others will pick up on some of what I'm saying here and take it further. We'll see. The most important thing to get across here is that no human being has ever imagined anything close to what life continuing is like. 'Heaven' is not for sissies," he said with a smile. "So what do *you* want to know about this place called 'heaven'?"

"Thanks, Josh. I guess I'm thinking more along the lines of what will we *do* in the next life?" I could be very naïve and a bit simpleminded, I guess (I hate to admit that), but I really wanted to hear something that I (and hopefully many others) could really latch on to and understand.

"Anything you can imagine doing. What are you passionate about? Whatever you *love* doing in this life, you can do in the next. And you will develop new passions. The only thing that can hold you back from doing whatever you want to do is your *imagination*."

The first thought that came to my mind was, "*Hmmm* . . . I've always been pretty passionate about sex. You mean we can—"

Just then there was a loud knocking on my apartment door. Oh, yeah, the pizza guy. Suddenly it dawned on me—I didn't have any money! I turned to Joshua, and with a kind of wild look in my eyes, I said to him, "Man, I didn't even think about how to pay for this stuff. Do you happen to have any dough?"

Yeah, we need some dough for the pizza guy.

The pizza guy knocked again, this time more insistently. Joshua said, "No need to panic. I've got this."

I opened the door, and the almost-exasperated pizza guy came in and handed me our pizza along with a dozen chicken wings and three cans of Coke. I turned to Joshua as if to say, "Now what?"

He turned to the pizza guy and asked, "Do you have a ten-dollar bill? Can I just borrow it for a second?" Confused, the pizza guy dug around in his fanny pack and pulled out a ten-dollar bill. Joshua took it, turned around, and lowering his head, said something under his breath. Was he *praying*? Praying for *what*? That the delivery guy would leave without asking for money? But when he turned back, Joshua handed the guy his original ten-dollar bill and then gave him fifty dollars on top of that! What the . . . ? The pizza guy was totally impressed with this sleight of hand, or whatever it was. He backed out into the hallway with a smile on his face and said an enthusiastic "Thanks!" before heading back toward the elevator down the hallway.

Now I was thinking, "What the hell just happened?"

Joshua took the pizza from me, and Joe grabbed the wings and Cokes.

"Anybody hungry?"

Really? Anybody hungry? "Can you tell me just what the hell just happened?" I asked him.

"Yeah, we needed some money, so I asked my Dad, and he gave me money, at least enough to pay for our pizza."

Plus a healthy tip, I figured. At least Jesus Christ wasn't cheap. Then I asked him, "Really? Is it that easy for you? You just ask for something, and your Dad gives it to you?" I was thinking, "Well, he is adopted, so maybe his Dad spoils him a bit."

"He doesn't spoil me, Rog. As I told my disciples so many years ago, you should be able to do anything I can do. After all, he's *your* Dad too."

"You know, Josh, it just started today to think of calling him my 'Dad.' I feel as though I'm really getting to think of him as my Dad ever since I heard you talking about him as *your* Dad. You're really making me think about my dysfunctional relationship with God."

"That's so cool!" Joshua said emphatically.

"Yeah, you're making me think back on how God has been helping me lately, even though I haven't been paying much attention to him. Sometimes it's the really small stuff that I notice, like getting Netflix from our neighbor for free."

"Good for you. Maybe we should eat first and pick up the thread of what we're talking about afterward."

After eating and clearing off the table, we continued with the interview.

Chapter Forty-Nine

For some reason, eating something seemed to give me some much-needed energy.

"You seemed to be saying before we ate that the Kingdom of God message was meant for everyone. My question is this: How does the Kingdom of God message apply to people of other faiths, like Muslims, for example? I mean, I could start listing the names of other religions, but it would be a long list."

"I taught the truth about God by means of stories and parables, but when you think of it, my whole life was a living parable in itself, don't you think?" he asked.

"Yeah, I do. It makes sense when you put it that way."

"The character of a person is validated by the kind of life that person lives. In my case, that includes the way I met death. The hardest thing in life for any of us is to continue on trusting that God is there when we're faced with suffering and pain and tragedy. In that sense, I was an example of innocent suffering. So the good news is that God is real; he loves every human being without any conditions, he deals with what Christians call 'sin' by forgiving it, and he will welcome all people into his Kingdom."

"So then, is there a hell?" I had wanted to ask him this earlier, but I forgot. Now it seemed like a good time to find out.

"No," he said, "there is no hell. The Christian concept of hell did not exist until nearly five hundred years after my death. By that time the so-called apostle Paul's version of Christianity had become the official religion of the Roman Empire. Christianity was still competing with many other Roman mystery religions, and the developing Christian hierarchy's biggest fear was that new converts might abandon Christianity in favor of one of these other religions. That would mean a loss of control, power, and money for the church. So the bishops and priests convened a council and decided to 'create' the idea of hell so as to keep their followers in line. They told the masses that Christianity was the one and only way to God and that anyone who believed in another religion would be damned to hell for eternity. The belief in hell has worked well for the Christian churches, especially the Catholic Church. It gave the pope, the bishops, and the priests great power over the masses. That power continues in the present day. But what does God think of the idea of hell? I can tell you firsthand that the idea of hell is immoral and obscene."

"I always thought that the idea that a loving God would even create a place like hell was, well, screwed up. But I never really said that to anyone because I was afraid of going to hell!"

"Now *that's* screwed up, Rog. And yet, throughout the centuries, that's why many people turn to Christianity—because they're afraid of going to hell. To believe that the God of the universe would create a place where anyone who didn't believe in him in the right way, which means the Christian way, would be punished and tortured forever is the most hateful, obscene teaching that has developed in Christianity. As history shows us, though, it worked and continues to work for the church. Fear is a great motivator for keeping people in line. It also works to persuade people to become Christians, so they can avoid going to hell. Such thinking makes my Dad look like a monster."

He was really into it now, as were Joseph and I, so I just sat back and listened.

"The way most Christians believe, it's as if only Christians, and by that I mean certain *kinds* of Christians, will ever get to this place you guys call 'heaven.' An attitude of arrogance is rampant among Christians. And how do you think God feels when mere human beings, no matter how smart they think they are, figure they have the mind of God all neatly figured out?"

"Okay, so for people of other faiths, can you sum it up in a nutshell?" I asked.

"Yeah, I can. I want to make it clear that God's reality is that all human beings will continue to live after this life on earth."

"Yes, I get that," I said. "But there's still some kind of bottom line, isn't there? Something about believing in God as some kind of basis or foundation for entering his Kingdom?" I asked.

"No," he answered. *"Living life to the fullest each day* is what's important, not merely believing in a set of doctrines and dogmas about me or God. Living your life to the best of your ability and helping others is what is important. And when you fall, pick yourself up, dust yourself off, and know that you're forgiven. Then move on. God had it all figured out long ago. Ever since the first self-conscious humans evolved, my Dad figured he was going to need help getting his message about the importance of peace, justice, and compassion across to them. He has sent many, many people in *all* the faith traditions to show people how to live meaningful lives. And then, at the time in human history he figured you guys needed it most, he chose me to show people what he's really like and how he thinks. He chose me to live and teach about the Kingdom of God. That's reality; that is true. And when I presented myself to my followers after my resurrection, they knew then that what I had taught about God and life was true. What I taught was a message of hope to all people of all times everywhere: *don't be afraid.* Trust in God for everything. Treat other people as you want to be treated. Be kindhearted, compassionate, and caring. Forgive anyone who causes you harm. But perhaps most important, *don't be afraid.*"

Talking about people of other faiths, and those with no faith, made me think of a related question.

"Is there such thing as a 'final judgment'?"

"No," he said, "There is no final judgment, no condemnation, no hell, and no punishment. God does not want any human being to miss out on all the cool stuff he has waiting for people after their bodies housing their personalities die."

I took off my glasses and wiped away the cobwebs of fatigue.

"Over the centuries there have been lots of different beliefs about what happens after one dies. The belief that eventually *all* creation, and all human beings, will be reconciled with God is the closest to the truth. God's Dream is for everyone to continue living. And he will make his Dream come true. In saying that, I don't mean that it will be simple. In fact, life after death is very complex. I don't know what else to say about the next life other than what I've already told you. God will make his Dream come true. The only thing you need to focus on is living this life to the fullest every day."

Chapter Fifty

I grabbed my pack of cigarettes off the kitchen table and fired one up. Joshua and Joseph followed my lead. After a couple of drags, I looked up at both of them and said, "I love smoking. I know it's bad for my health, but I don't think I'll regret it. I've always enjoyed smoking. You guys?" I asked.

Joshua and Joseph looked at each other and burst into laughter.

After they regained their composure, Joseph jumped in, "Yeah, I get what you mean. Smoking is kind of disgusting, but in a good way."

"In a good way? I don't get it," I said.

Joshua picked up where Joseph left off. "It's tough being human—believe me, Rog, I get that. And humans are notorious for doing things that are harmful to their health or whatever, but they still do it anyway. Goes with the territory, so to speak. I really don't have much of a comment on smoking. Drinking, smoking, doing drugs, being a nice guy, being a prick—it's all up to you. You can screw yourself up and, by extension, cause loved ones and other people grief as well, but that's where having free will, the power to make your own decisions, comes in. Can you think of a better way?"

"A better way of what?" I asked.

"Of living, of being alive."

"I guess not, but it seems like the *big* things in life aren't our decisions anyway. Like we talked about earlier, who our parents are, where we're born, our upbringing—stuff like that."

"True. But just thinking about *now,* today, do you feel like you have the freedom to make your own decisions?"

I had to think about that.

"Yeah, I do, for the most part. I mean, there are still things in life that I don't really feel like I have any control over, but I do believe, from what you've told me today, Josh, that I can *decide* to be happy despite my personal circumstances and that I can decide to live my life to the fullest every day, trusting God for my well-being and helping others who are less fortunate than I am! How about *that*?"

"You're catching on, dude; you're catching on."

Chapter Fifty-One

I said, "Okay, Josh, my next question is, why did you have to die such a horrific death? Why did you have to die at all? Wouldn't you have preferred to live to a ripe old age with a wife, children, and grandchildren scampering around?"

"Yes, if it had been up to me, I would have chosen to live. But let me start by telling you what my death *wasn't* about. If you listen to most Christians today, you get the distinct impression that I died on the cross for every individual 'sin' that has ever been committed by every person and that ever *would* be committed. And those same Christians would then try to connect some non-existing dots by saying that's how one is 'saved,' by merely 'believing' that and 'accepting Christ' into their hearts, whatever that means."

Joshua really was the farthest thing from what many would consider to be a Christian. But to be fair, he wasn't a Christian anyway.

"And it certainly wasn't about God requiring some sort of blood sacrifice to atone for people's 'sins.' I'll tell you one thing, though, about what my death says to human beings: *no more sacrifices*!" It pains both me and my Dad to think of all the blood, both of animals and humans, that has been spilled over the centuries in order to somehow 'appease' my Dad's sense of 'righteousness.' The whole concept of blood sacrifice is designed by men."

"But in the Bible, it says that—"

"Never mind what it says in the Bible. I'm talking in real terms here. It's been repugnant to my Dad and me from the beginning and remains repugnant today. I died to put an end to all that. God wanted to put an end to the madness of offering sacrifices to him for good. No more sacrifices needed to establish friendship between human beings and God."

"There go a bunch of hymns out the window," I said.

"I guess. I mean, if people hold to the belief that I am God, then they believe that I was the 'sacrificial lamb' and that my death somehow mysteriously absolves people of their sins once and for all; it would mean that one of the 'persons' of God died to somehow appease another 'person' of the Godhead—in this case, my Dad. Me dying by crucifixion, dying at all, really, shines a light on God's reality. Like, few people would disagree that the foundation of Christian life and belief is that I was the second person of Trinity and that I came to earth in human form, was crucified, died, and was buried. Then God raised me from the dead. But that I *did* die and that I *was* raised from the dead by God, that my trust in him was validated, that God's love was shown to be stronger than the bonds of mortality, and that all people can have a taste of the glory that God has in store for each and every person; well, that's pretty cool if you ask me."

I nodded in agreement and thought, "Yeah, pretty damn cool."

"Faith should be grounded in *reason* and *evidence*. Most people really don't know *why* they believe *what* they believe. For example, the belief that God raised me from the dead is based on evidence—what I like to call the *sociological fact*. No one disputes that; however, you try to spin it, *something* extraordinary happened within days of my death. After I was crucified and buried, all my followers turned tail and went into hiding—except for Mary Magdalene, my mom, and a few other women. All the men who called themselves my disciples hid behind locked doors in fear of their lives. Like, who wants to be crucified? So with all their hopes and dreams smashed on the rocks, within a few *days* after my death, you find that my disciples were out in the streets claiming to have seen *me*! Many were thrown into prison, and some even put to death, but nothing could stop them after they had seen me alive again. I appeared to them in visions, with the same kind of body that all will have after they ditch this physical one. And within a few short years, they had pretty much turned the world upside down."

"Few would argue that I was fully human, even those Christians who believe that I was also fully God. I was so scared while I was on the cross, knowing that I was going to die. I even asked God, 'Please, *please,* God, I don't want to die!' Then God raised me from the dead in the same way that he raises all people to life after they have died and has been doing for thousands of years. He chose me to *prove* to people that life continues after death. People aren't raised from the dead by some built-in immortality of the soul but by an act of God. This is not the same kind of body that I had before I died and realized myself that life continued after death."

"Most Christians believe that you were raised physically from the dead. Weren't you?"

"People throughout the centuries have had some pretty bizarre beliefs about what happened to me. I wasn't some resuscitated corpse that appeared to my disciples after I died. I appeared to them in visions. They recognized me and knew right then that death had no hold over me and, by extension, them. In their minds, I wasn't dead anymore. Seeing me empowered them and gave them the courage to continue on with my Kingdom of God movement in the face of persecution and death. After they saw me, they never wavered. The accounts of my resurrection in the Gospels make it appear that my corpse was brought back to life. It wasn't. God transformed my body in the same way he transforms *all* human beings after this earthly life, and I appeared to them in a series of vivid visions."

"So, to make sure I get this right, God raises to life every human being who has ever died and will die. Is that right?"

"Yes. *In the twinkling of an eye.*"

Chapter Fifty-Two

Joshua said, "No. We're going out, the three of us. I want you to take us downtown and show us around. I want to meet with people and engage them. Are you up for that?"

"No!" I said emphatically. "It's after midnight, and you want me to take you and Joseph *downtown*? No way, Josh. Sorry, but it's *way* too dangerous."

I lived in Chicago, and Joshua wanted me to take him and Joe to the South Side! At night? Homelessness was rampant, and the drug trade flourished There was no way we were going downtown at this hour.

"And I want us to take the bus."

Okay, so my wired mind was spinning. "I *have* to talk him out of this madness." Then it hit me. Joshua and Joseph could not be hurt, not with the indestructible body that Joshua had and Joseph being an angel.

But what about *me*? Traveling back in time was nerve wracking enough, but I *knew* what to expect in the downtown core.

"I have to talk him out of this!" I thought wildly.

Chapter Fifty-Three

I tried again. "Look, guys, the bus only comes by once an hour after midnight, so we might as well not even—"

Joshua cut me off by saying, "Let's go, then! Joe, get ready. C'mon, Rog, we have a bus to catch!"

Joshua started herding us into our shoes and jackets and out my apartment door.

Joshua shepherded us into the hallway to the elevator. There was no one around the main lobby, but I knew there would be plenty of people in the downtown core—the kind of people you didn't really want to hang out with, but . . . "The kind of people Jesus hung out with back in the day," I thought wildly. "But does he really understand what he's getting us into?" I wondered.

"Not to worry, Rog. Joe, run down to the corner and make sure we catch the bus."

Joseph took off jogging as Joshua and I struggled to stay up with him. Sure enough, Joseph made it to the bus stop just as the bus was stopped behind a red light on the other side of the street. Was it just good luck or . . . ?

No time to think. Joshua dug into the pocket of his jeans and, amazingly, pulled out the exact bus fare for three people! How we would get home I didn't want to think about, but after watching Joshua pay the pizza guy earlier in the evening, I told myself not to worry about it.

We were the only three passengers on the bus. We sat in silence for the next twenty minutes until the bus driver announced over the loudspeaker, "Next stop Elgin Street."

Elgin Street, the infamous stretch in the downtown core that was inhabited by drug dealers, crackheads, heroin addicts, pimps, working girls, and homeless people, the majority of whom lived as best they could with their respective, and usually quite serious, mental health issues, HIV, and hepatitis C.

I avoided visiting this part of the city. A few times over the years, some friends and I would walk along Elgin Street in broad daylight, checking out the vast assortment of characters (especially the working girls) and occasionally popping into one of the many head shops or small trinket shops. I always felt relatively safe there during the day, but I had never actually ventured to this downtown locale at night.

Yet here I was. As we got off the bus and began walking slowly down the street, we were immediately surrounded by street people of all ages and all genders. My only consolation was that I wasn't alone. And not only was I not alone but I was also walking with Jesus Christ and an angel of the Lord! What could possibly go wrong?

The dozen or so people who immediately surrounded us at the bus station were far from threatening. Most just asked if we had any spare change or cigarettes. I shook my head "no" and then watched with some unease as Joshua reached into the pocket of his jeans and produced a roll of what I quickly learned were twenty-dollar bills. He patiently began handing out twenties as more and more street people heard the ruckus and entered the fray for their share of the largesse. At one point he held a hand up, then reached into his jacket, and pulled out two packs of cigarettes. He handed the two packs to two guys in front of him. Instead of scampering away with their riches, they each took one out and passed the pack to someone else. That pattern continued as Joshua returned to passing out twenty-dollar bills.

I moved off to the side of the crowd while Joseph stood close to Joshua, gently directing people away from Joshua after they had received their money.

I watched in amazement for the next thirty minutes. I could see Joshua saying something to each person he handed a bill to;

he always made some kind of physical contact with each one too, sometimes just touching an outstretched hand and other times reaching out with his right hand to touch a head or an arm or a shoulder.

We didn't move on down the street until everyone who had approached him had a bill. Everyone was smiling and chattering away to their friends as they disengaged from the presence of Joshua and Joseph. No one paid me any attention.

Half an hour after we first arrived, we were able to start walking down the street with just a few following us. The street was crowded with a wide assortment of characters. We passed a trio of scantily clad young girls. I tried not to make eye contact or check them out. I mean, here I was with Jesus, and I didn't want him to think that I was a pervert.

But Joshua stopped right in front of them and moved close. Within seconds I saw that they were all laughing together, and one of the girls was doubled over with laughter. Jesus looked so at home with them. Joseph had come over to keep me company a few feet away. Joshua was telling them a story, I guessed, by his hand motions and their giggling. I so wished I could hear him, but I couldn't. The music from a nearby pub was blasting out into the street; *thumpa-thumpa* dance music that you could feel in your chest. I made a mental note to ask him what they were talking about when we got back to my apartment.

The four of them chatted for twenty minutes or so while Joseph and I watched the passersby and smoked cigarettes. Then the girls started walking down the street, motioning for Joshua to follow them. One of the girls caught my eye and motioned Joseph and I to follow too. I sidled up to Joshua as we walked. He leaned over and said in a loud voice, "We're going to a party!"

"Omigod," I thought. What was he getting us into?

We followed the girls as they snaked their way through the crowded sidewalk. Some people were walking in the street when they could, although cars and pickups rolled steadily by as if in slow motion, honking horns and guys yelling out to the many working girls by the curb.

The three girls we were following quickly ducked into a dark alley between two small shops. Joshua and Joseph were heading into the alley. I stopped and yelled to them, "Hey, guys, not in there! Let's stay on the street." They both stopped when I yelled over to them and then both peered into the alley. Against my better judgment, I made my way over to them at the entrance. I could barely see into the alley in the dim light, but I could make out a number of shapes—some standing, some sitting, all of them smoking cigarettes or whatever.

Joshua sensed my hesitation. "It's okay, Rog, I'll make sure you're safe," he said. "This is why I wanted to come down here tonight. These are my people. These are the same kind of people I hung out with when I was here back in the day."

Joseph nodded in agreement.

"Okay, Josh, I do trust you, but I feel very nervous going into that alley."

"Follow me," he said to Joseph and me.

So we did.

Chapter Fifty-Four

We moved slowly into the alley, stopping every few steps as our eyes adjusted to the dimness. After a few minutes, we could make out the shapes in the alley. There was a fire-escape ladder pulled down to ground level. We could see a dozen or so people sitting, standing, and smoking on it. The three girls we had been following were nowhere to be seen.

At the foot of the ladder was a young girl crumpled on the ground. Joshua knelt down to check her pulse. As he touched her, she jerked up, eyes wide and as big as saucers.

"Hey, don't touch me!" she said loudly.

A few heads turned our way but quickly lost interest. Joshua continued kneeling by her as Joseph and I stood a few feet away, watching.

"What do you want, man? I'll give you a blow job for fifty bucks," she said to Joshua.

Joseph and I took a few steps closer so that we could hear clearly.

Joshua said to her, "No, my child, I'm here to heal you."

Heal her? I wondered how *that* was going to go over.

She answered him with what I expected. "Heal me from *what*?" she asked.

"From yourself," he said quietly, with a tone of compassion. She was now in a sitting position, and Joshua was still kneeling next to her.

"Look, man, I need a hit. Do you have any crack?"

"If I gave you crack," he responded, "you would be in the same position you are now in a few hours. I have something better than crack. I want to take away your addiction and make you whole again."

She looked into his eyes and burst into tears. Sobbing, she was barely understandable. "I'm so screwed up, man. There's no help for me." She lowered her eyes as she regained her composure. "I've tried everything. My body craves it, and I'm so sick and tired of being sick and tired all the time," she said amid her tears.

Joshua reached out and put his hand on her head. She didn't object.

"Do you want to be healed?" he asked her.

"Yes, if you have the power, I would."

"I have the power," Joshua said. He held her chin in his left hand, looked straight into her watery eyes, and said, "Be healed."

Joseph and I were transfixed. Would he really heal her of her crack addiction? How would we even know if she was healed?

The answer came quickly.

She stood up from where she was sitting in the dim alley, turned to Joshua, and threw her arms around him. She was shorter than he was, so she wrapped her arms around his torso, sobbing uncontrollably. Joshua held her tightly and stroked her hair.

"It's okay; it's okay," he kept repeating to her. After a minute he added, "God has taken away your addiction. You won't have to perform sexual favors for money anymore. Go home and change your life. God will help you."

Joseph and I were close enough to see her whole visage change from sadness and despair to joy and gratitude.

"Are you God?" she asked Joshua.

"No," he said. "But there is a God, and he loves you to death. Try to remember him every morning when you wake up and thank him for healing you."

"But I can't go home," she said. "My parents won't have anything to do with me."

"They will now. They love you deeply, and they will take you in and keep you safe."

She believed him. "Can you help me get home?" she asked.

"Yes," Joshua responded. "Do you have a cell phone?"

"Yes," she said. "The guy who took me in and now pimps me out gave me one so he could keep track of me."

"Then call a taxi and have it pick you up in front of the alley. Don't worry, I'll pay him."

"I don't know what to say, sir. What's your name, anyway?"

"Uh . . . Joshua."

"Thank you, thank you, thank you, Joshua! I'll never forget what you did for me."

She pulled out her cell phone as she headed back to the entrance of the alley. We watched her stand there by herself for five minutes. The taxi came, and she was gone.

Joseph and I drew close to Joshua. People were still all around the alley and on the fire escape. I looked at him, about to ask what had happened.

He said first, "No questions, Rog. You saw and heard what happened. It is what it is."

For some reason I was fine with it. He was right. What was there to say?

Chapter Fifty-Five

Joshua glanced up the fire-escape ladder and said, "Follow me," as he began quickly climbing the stairs to a door on the second floor.

Loud dance music was booming through the door into the night as we entered a large loft full of people dancing, smoking, shooting up, and just hanging out. Lots of laughter and chatting, but sad sights everywhere: several bodies sprawled on the floor by the walls and one girl shooting what I figured was heroin, sitting cross-legged and frustrated as she kept jabbing for a vein.

"Was Joshua going to heal them all?" I asked Joseph in a loud whisper.

Joseph looked at me and whispered back in a hoarse voice, "I don't think so. I don't know. He's not tame, you know. He's unpredictable."

Joshua glanced around the room and stopped in his tracks. There by the DJ sound stage stood a tall man, bare chested and muscular, completely covered in tattoos depicting what looked like ancient symbols: a dragon, various colored snakes with fangs, and his shaved head tattooed with dark red-and-black images of . . . I couldn't tell from where I was standing. He was talking animatedly with a petite working girl. As if on cue, his head jerked up and sideways as he caught Joshua staring at him. They locked eyes, and there was a palpable tension between them. Then the guy turned his head in my direction. His eyes looked totally red to me, and I took a step backward even though he was yards away from the three of us. He looked quickly at Joseph as though sizing him up and then locked eyes with Joshua again.

I held my breath as the guy began to charge through the crowd toward us, eyes on fire and pushing away people in front of him with brute force. The tattooed man reached us and began walking a slow circle around us as those closest to us scampered away. Thick puffs of smoke drifted up toward the skylight in the ceiling, making him appear ethereal. Joshua turned his gaze to the knife the guy had suddenly proffered—a dagger with an ornate handle. The man's eyes were wide and red, and he seemed to be in a demonic trance.

I suddenly realized that I was going to die in that room tonight.

But instead he lunged at Joshua with a growl, looking to embed the knife deep into his chest. At the last second, Joseph reacted. In an instant a bright ray of light shot from his eyes into the face of the tattooed man. Momentarily blinded, the man raised his left hand to cover his eyes as the knife pierced Joshua's chest. Joshua went down.

"Omigod!" my mind screamed. Was Joshua dead?

Joseph wrenched the man's knife arm and snapped it like a twig. The man didn't seem to notice. Joseph quickly grabbed the man's head between his two hands and gave it a powerful twist, snapping the man's neck. He went down in a heap, the room filled with the screaming of the shocked crowd. The music had stopped, and people began running wildly for the lone exit leading to the fire escape.

Joseph and I turned to the fallen Joshua. Joseph knelt down and checked his neck for a pulse.

"What the heck?" I thought wildly. "Did the tattooed man actually kill Jesus Christ? Again?" I was beside myself.

Joseph took his hand away from Joshua's neck and turned his head to look me straight in the eye.

"Do you pray, man?" he asked. "Because I need your help, and fast."

"Pray? What the . . . ? Right now? Joseph needs me to *pray*?" I thought. I had no idea how that would help.

"It will, Rog. Can you do that for me?"

"Okay," I said. "What should I—"

"Just *pray*!" he shouted at me in the now-empty room. I could hear sirens off in the distance.

"Okay, okay," I thought. "I can do this." It's not like I never talked to God. I did on occasion, and I knew that this meeting with Jesus, this interview, the past eighteen or so hours now, were changing my life. I could *feel* it inside. And now . . . now I was needed!

I was already kneeling, so as I kept my eyes on an unconscious Joshua lying on the ground with the knife jammed to the hilt in his chest. I prayed, "God, uh . . . Dad, can you see us here? Your son is in trouble! Please, please, we need your help."

And that was it. I didn't know what else to say.

"I'm here, Rog," a voice whispered in my ear. "*Omigod*! Is that . . . ?"

I quickly noticed it was Joshua who whispered to me. I looked down at Joshua and—his eyelids slowly opened! He was alive! I said a quick "Thank you!" to God as Joseph slowly lifted Joshua into a sitting position.

"You okay, Lord?" Joseph whispered. We were both ecstatic. "He is Risen!" I thought stupidly. But he was.

"Yeah, I think so. Joe, can you pull the knife out?"

Joseph took hold of the hilt of the knife and pulled it out quickly. Joshua lifted his T-shirt to his neck. There was a puncture wound in his chest but no blood.

All three of us instinctively glanced at the tattooed man lying on the ground with a broken neck. He was dead.

"Man, I didn't expect that," Joshua murmured. "I should have, though."

Joseph and I helped Joshua to his feet. Joshua lifted his T-shirt again, and the puncture wound was gone.

"Thanks, Joe, and thank you, Rog, for getting my Dad's attention."

"Really?" I thought. "My little prayer actually *did* something?"

"Yeah, it did. That's how it works. You just have to ask sometimes."

Joshua pulled his shirt down and put a hand on each of our shoulders.

"Let's go home," he said simply.

Chapter Fifty-Six

We rode home in silence. I wanted to ask Joshua questions, but I knew it wasn't the time.

I had regained my composure after arriving back at my apartment. My thoughts were crystallized. I *had* to find out what had happened downtown!

"No, Rog, you were there. You saw what happened. You can think about it after we're done. But for now, let's get back to the interview."

I didn't know if I could. But I sensed that Joshua was going to leave it up to me to figure out.

Chapter Fifty-Seven

When we were back in our places around the kitchen table, I gathered my notes and said, "Okay, Josh, I think I'm ready." I took a deep breath, exhaled, and said, "My next question may be the most-asked question in the twenty-first century, maybe even since the dawn of time. According to the most recent World Health Organization statistics, nine million children under the age of five die each year from preventable causes, usually because of the lack of clean drinking water. So my question is this: How does God fit into the picture? Why is there so much needless pain and suffering in the world today? I'm sorry, Josh, but this is one of the things that haunts me and holds me back from totally trusting God. Can you talk about this?"

"Yes, and let me say at the start that the reality of unnecessary pain and suffering around the world today and since the arrival of human beings on the earth has caused God unimaginable grief."

"So God grieves?"

"All human beings grieve, and we're all evolving into God's image; so yes, God's heart, so to speak, breaks when he sees needless suffering and pain in the world. It is perhaps the biggest stumbling block to belief in God. Here is where I would encourage you to begin. No human being has come up with a satisfactory answer to the question of needless pain and suffering in the world. But that doesn't mean there *isn't* one. You can compare this with what we encounter in the physical universe: just because we can't explain the mysteries of the universe doesn't mean that there *are* no explanations."

"Yeah, yeah, but *you* must know the answer. And if you don't, certainly *God* must know."

The emotion in my voice was electric. Here I was talking with Jesus Christ, and I could foresee that whatever he had to say about this issue would be frustrating.

Joshua knew this.

"Can you imagine a world other than this one?" he asked.

"Yes!" I answered emphatically. "I can! I can imagine a world where people are kind to one another and who love compassionately and who really care about helping one another. That's not the way it is now, but I can *imagine* it."

"Yet what you imagine may be less appealing than you think at first. You know the reality: there *is* unimaginable suffering and pain in the world. One cause is a human one; what we see happening in parts of Africa and many other parts of the world is caused by men in positions of political power and making decisions that affect their respective populations—decisions that invariably support their own self-interests. You guys have the technology to produce clean drinking water anywhere in the world. All it takes is the political, social, and religious will to do so."

"Okay, but we *do* have people and organizations all over the world that have stood up to injustice that leads to needless suffering, starvation, and lack of clean drinking water and speak out about human apathy toward those who suffer needlessly."

"Yes, and God works closely with those people, organizations, and voices. I understand that merely saying that everything will be understood and connected and wonderful in God's Kingdom in the future is not enough. "

"Yeah, everything will be so wonderful," I said, with more than a hint of sarcasm. "And I *do* believe that, I guess, but it doesn't really help us while we're going through this thing called 'life.'"

"Okay, then, try to imagine a world where there is no unnecessary suffering and even no dying, no death. Knowing what we know about human nature and the reality that we could live in a world where we can do and think whatever we want, what do you imagine *that* kind of world would be like?"

I wasn't quite sure where he was going with this, but I gave it a try.

"Yeah, I think I can. It would be a world where people would pursue their own self-interests and satisfy their heart's desire without having to worry about causing other people to suffer or being punished or even dying.

"Wait," I caught myself. "That doesn't sound very good, actually. I could imagine that kind of world being worse than this one!"

"Good for you, Rog. So you have two options, two worlds, in front of you: one world with no suffering or death, just doing whatever you want and not having to worry about other people, or a world that you currently live in where there is the *possibility* of trying to overcome pain and suffering with real love and compassion and making choices that matter, both to others and to God."

"What about a third option: imagining a world where everyone truly cares for the concerns of others?"

"Yes, a third option. Can you imagine that kind of world? Is it possible that God can? Is it God's Dream for a world like that?"

It began to dawn on me that, yes, I could imagine a world that was *beyond* my understanding, *beyond* my grasp as a human being bound to this material world.

"I *can* imagine some future existence beyond this earthly journey where injustice and suffering don't exist. Otherwise, God didn't get it right. But this present world is so unfair to so many people who suffer that it cries out for ultimate justice. And while that may never happen here on earth, I can imagine it happening in some future time; that is, if there *is* a God of compassion and justice, which I choose to believe there is."

Joshua was looking at me intently with what I took to be compassion in his eyes.

"Every human being now and in the past," he said, "has felt a tug of unfinished business in his or her heart—a very real sense of injustice that needs to be corrected and of suffering that needs to be explained or compensated. That yearning that there is something more, something yet to come, reflects God's image, God's Dream, in every human being. One can try and dismiss it or ignore it or pretend he or she doesn't feel it, but it's there in everyone."

I quickly grabbed for my pack of cigarettes. Just as quickly, Joshua reached out and held my arm.

"Look at me, Rog. From ancient times to the present, human beings *want* to believe—in God, in themselves, in love, and in an afterlife. There is no answer to needless pain and suffering on this side of the veil. There is only a *response*: what can you do as an individual or as part of a community or organization or a church or a mosque, or whatever, to help those who suffer or are in pain or who have tremendous need in their lives. You have your time and whatever extra money you may have and your love and compassion. There's no need to be angry with God for what happens in this life."

I felt ashamed. Why was I so angry with *God* for all the needless suffering and misery in the world? What about just worrying about my own little world, my family and friends and those in need who I interact with? Where was all this anger coming from?

"Don't beat yourself up, Rog. You're trying to figure out God's reality, and that is a virtue. I just think you might want to consider cutting him a little slack when it comes to the suffering and tragedy you see in the world around you. Learn to rejoice at whoever and whatever encourages people to become aware of God and who want to share in God's Dream. We're all in this together."

"I *do* get it, Josh. I *want* to be aware of God in my life and to be compassionate and loving to others. Being with you today, I feel like a blind man regaining the gift of sight. I will do better at encouraging and helping others however I can and being humble before God and others."

I lowered my head into my hands and started sobbing.

Joshua got up from his chair, came over to me, and embraced me awkwardly. I stood up, and we hugged each other tightly.

"My God," I thought through my tears, "what is happening to me?"

Chapter Fifty-Eight

It took me some time to regain my composure. "Okay, Josh, before we run out of time, can we talk about the white elephant in the room?"

"The white elephant? So you must be wanting to know what I think about sex."

"Yeah, okay. It's just that I don't know of any person who really has ever figured it out," I said.

"You're right, Rog. It *is* the most powerful thing that God created for human beings. First I'm going to remind you of this: you and all people before you were created in God's image. I want you to think about that while I pour myself a cup of coffee. Can you do that for me?"

"Yes, I can, and I will," I promised.

Joshua got up to get more coffee while I sat there kind of stunned. I had never really connected the dots that sex and all that goes with it was part of being created in God's image. What did that say about God? I hadn't even designed a question for Joshua, and he was already back and sitting down.

"I know. It's a tough one. Let me start by going back to how I responded to situations back in the day when people were accused of sexual impropriety. My attitude to the accused was always one of compassion and understanding, because I knew how powerful sex was. I had my own temptations many times when I was here before. It is just *so* powerful. It's pretty clear that I hung out with down-and-out people, the mentally ill, the diseased, the physically deformed, working girls, alcoholics, drug addicts, and many more. So much so that rumors were abundant about me. I was accused of being a wino and a glutton. And worse. I was accused many times of being 'sinful' because I hung out with that crowd—and especially accused of being friendly with working girls. It kind of bugged me at first that the ones who recorded my story actually included that in their Gospels. But now I'm glad they did. It certainly shows that I was human, wouldn't you agree?"

"Yeah, I see what you mean," I said. I mean, I *kind* of did.

"Everyone knows the story about the woman caught in the act of adultery in John's Gospel. It's a made-up story that a zealous scribe inserted into the text a century after I lived, but the story really reflects my attitude toward sex. As the author of the Gospel of John tells it, I told her that I didn't judge her or condemn her. And why not? Because God doesn't condemn her. I had tons to say about people who were hypocrites, or pathological liars, or who talked about what a 'good' person they were. In Mark's Gospel he listed sexual misdemeanors together with being envious and self-centered and, in particular, proud. The other thing is that God's response to sexual impropriety is the same as it is for any other act of selfishness: *he forgives it.* People have to suffer the consequences of their decisions, which can be disastrous and very hurtful to others. But I never laid down any kind of code about sexual conduct. I just never thought it was all that important to make public comments about sex—like for those who are single, or engaged, or widowed, or gay or lesbian, or couples facing an unwanted pregnancy."

"Wow, I just thought of more questions about sex," I said.

"We'll get to whatever you want to ask, Rog. But by not commenting on sexual conduct, that doesn't mean that I believe that anyone should just sleep around without thinking about it or being compassionate and empathetic toward other people. And I'm with most humans who have lived on this earth in that I really do get angry and feel a sense of hatred about cases of rape or child abuse or human trafficking. But that's not what we're talking about right now."

"We *should,* though," I added.

"Maybe, but it's not at the top of my priority list for this interview with limited time—know what I mean?" he asked.

"I do, Josh; I do. I just know that readers of this interview would be so anxious to hear more about what you and your Dad think about this stuff."

"Yeah, all human types throughout history have always had sex on their minds. I mean, as I said earlier, it's such a powerful force that we're just conditioned as human beings to think about it a lot and to do it whenever we can, right?"

"Yeah," I agreed. "Just *one* more thing, though, okay?"

Chapter Fifty-Nine

I should say from the outset that I know quite a few gay people. I even lived with a gay man for a year and was the richer for it. No conflicts, no intrusions into my privacy. He was a really good guy.

Joshua read my mind. "Okay, you want to know if being gay or lesbian is okay with my Dad."

"Uh, yeah, basically," I said.

Joshua was looking down at his hands.

"So let's start with the obvious. God created the climate for all kinds of humans to evolve throughout what you guys call 'human history.' And to state it in plain terms, the way humans have evolved is part of the natural order and based on natural selection—most as heterosexual and some as homosexual, just like what we see in thousands and thousands of other species. As uncomfortable you may think it is to be attracted to another man, you still want to try to understand, right? And part of that understanding is trying to look at the whole 'gay' orientation from the perspective of someone who is gay."

I nodded in agreement. "So do you agree that all Christians should welcome gays and lesbians into their churches and that they be allowed to get married and that kind of stuff?"

"You sound a bit uncomfortable with this topic," Joshua said.

"Yeah, I guess I am," I said uncomfortably.

"Look, Rog, this is a contentious issue for most Christians, as well as for those of different faith traditions. The history of behavior toward gays and lesbians is replete with violence and prejudice and all sorts of atrocities, many of those views and behaviors being done in my name! Can you imagine how I feel about that? Or how my Dad feels?"

"No, I can't," I said.

"So the thing is, I'm telling you as clearly as I can: God set in motion the evolutionary process—some people with a same-sex orientation, some people with autism, or male pattern baldness, or whatever. And the right way to relate to gays and lesbians is the same way that you should related to *every* human being—with love and compassion, integrity, respect, and empathy."

"Okay, so you're saying that being gay is a natural part of the human experience?" I asked.

"Yes, it is. Most Christians, both Catholic and Protestant, believe that homosexuality is a lifestyle choice. That's loopy thinking. Yes, the Bible condemns homosexuality, but that merely reflects primitive Bronze Age thinking. It goes back to taking the Bible as the 'Word of God.' Many Christian leaders today, including the pope, believe that this issue is *the* key issue today. That is, if homosexuality gains acceptance by Christians, then the Bible is undermined to the point where even Christians would have to concede that it is *not* the infallible 'Word of God.' And Christian leaders cannot allow that to happen. It would mean the end of the line as far as biblical authority goes."

"There's a story in the Bible about how David, before he was anointed king of Israel, loved the king's son Jonathan 'more than he loved women.' In this story, we have to ask ourselves the question: Can two people of the same sex have a loving, committed relationship with God's favor? The answer is 'yes,' because Jonathan and David did, and even according to the Bible, God celebrates their relationship. Remember that David is called 'a man after God's own heart' in the Bible. He was one of Israel's best-loved kings. He is one of the most prolific writers of scripture. He is in my lineage, and *he loved Jonathan more than he loved women.*"

"If that story is true, it sheds a whole new light on the whole homosexual experience in the context of the Jewish and Christian belief systems, as well as to many, if not *all,* religions in the world."

"This is a story that really happened, Rog. Most Christians spin their relationship to be about male bonding. But it's not. It's about God blessing a same-sex relationship. Until Christians begin accepting the LGBT community around the world as natural and healthy, Christianity will continue to promote discrimination, hate, and intolerance. I'm hoping that making this clear in this interview will go a long way toward changing the deep-seated Christian mind-set about homosexuality."

"I'm wondering, too, Josh, about why most Christians around the world, as exemplified by the Roman Catholic Church and evangelical Christians, are so adamant about condemning same-sex relationships as a heinous sin to the point that LGBT people are not welcome into those churches and are so openly and vociferously condemned."

"Christianity today is a house of cards, Rog. You pull out one card of the foundation, and the whole thing comes tumbling down. In this case, the Bible is that card. Most Christians believe that the Bible is the 'Word of God,' infallible, containing no errors and coming straight from the mouth of God. It's fair to say that homosexuality is explicitly condemned in the Bible in both the Old and New Testaments. So, the thinking goes, *God himself* condemns homosexuality and therefore condemns human beings who engage in homosexual behavior. And that's the crux of the matter. If homosexuality is deemed acceptable by the Roman Catholic and evangelical branches of Christianity, then the Bible is wrong on this issue. And if it's wrong on homosexuality, then what else might it be wrong about? See what I mean? Accepting homosexuality would bring the whole house of cards down because the Bible would be seen as fallible and prone to error."

"I hear you, dude, and you've already said earlier in this interview that the Bible is just plain wrong on other issues too, right?"

"Right. As I said, the Bible merely reflects Bronze Age thinking from one ethnic tribal group, the Jews. But no orthodox Christian can permit that kind of thinking because it undermines the whole sense of the God of the universe writing a book for all human beings to follow word for word and taken literally. Christianity as we know it would become obsolete and meaningless. That's my hope."

"Okay," I said, "I get it that you aren't a big supporter of Christianity, or any religion for that matter, but don't you think . . . well, aren't you worried that when people read this interview, you might destroy their faith or at least start to doubt what they believe?"

"Yes, yes! That's exactly what I'd like to see. Most Christians, most followers of any organized religion, don't have a clue *why* they believe what they do. Most people either stay in the religion they were brought up in or spend the rest of their lives trying to get *out*. I'm here to set the record straight, not just about Christianity, but about religion in general. It's time for the next step in human evolution, to rely on reason and common sense and evidence and facts rather than just blindly following what your religious leaders tell you to believe. God is real. He cares for every individual. Now throw off your chains of blind faith and become *aware* of who he is and how much he loves you. Learn to live your life to the fullest every day, being aware of God's presence in your lives, treating others the way you would like to be treated, and helping others whenever you can. Every day is an adventure. Live that adventure!"

Chapter Sixty

I said, "Okay, Josh, I know we're almost out of time, but I want to ask you about the whole gender thing, both in Christianity and many other religions throughout history. In my experience, no matter how Christians try to spin it, women have always been regarded as second-class citizens, at best, from a Christian perspective. So my question is, what's your take on the whole gender issue in Christianity?"

Joshua had a sad look on his face as he took a moment to gather his thoughts.

"You're right, Rog, and I'm glad you brought this up. Even a rudimentary knowledge of the Bible reveals that women have never been regarded as equals to men. Even today that attitude persists, although in more subtle ways than in the past. In the Bible, with rare exceptions, women are regarded and treated as inferior to men, often as little more than property. But the Bible is a book by and for men. Women had little status and few rights. Even the God of the Bible is male. True, I taught that we should refer to God as our Father, but I was merely trying to get across the idea of 'God as Parent' to a patriarchal audience. God is neither male nor female. The healthiest way to think of him is as both father and mother.

"Take polygamy, for example. According to the Bible, men were permitted and even blessed by God to have as many wives and sex slaves as they could afford, but no woman was allowed to have more than one husband. A man was permitted to sell his daughter if he needed money—allow his daughter to be raped for money—and to divorce his wife for any number of trivial reasons. And that's really just the tip of the iceberg. Most Christians are well aware of Paul of Tarsus's demands that women must keep silent during a church service, must not be allowed to teach or prophecy, and to be 'subservient' to her husband. How's *that* for status?"

I knew all this from my time at Bible college and from talking with Christians over the years, but I wanted Joshua to articulate his views on women for the record.

"No reasonable person can deny that the Bible portrays women as inferior to men. Islam and Judaism are no better. It's a travesty, and there's no end in sight as long as men continue to believe that the God of the universe wrote a book just for them. I applaud the advances that women have made to regain their position as equal to men, but there's really no end in sight as long as religion persists.

"Look at the story of Jeptha in the Bible. Jeptha was the commander of the Israeli army when faced with an attack from the Ammonites. Jeptha made an agreement with God that he would offer up the first living thing to walk through the door of his house as a burnt offering to God if he would give him this military victory. Jeptha had many sons and daughters. As sick as this story is, I believe it's important to hear it. Sure enough, Jeptha defeated the Ammonites. Upon his return home, the first living thing to walk through the door of his house to greet him was his teenage daughter. He was assuming that it would be a chicken or a dog. Jeptha was horrified but thanked God that at least it wasn't one of his sons. But in his mind, a deal is a deal. True to his word, he offered his daughter up to God as a human sacrifice, dedicating her to God. Even more shocking is that God *accepted* his sacrifice. This story clearly reveals both the male mentality as well as the cruelty of the God of the Bible. And this is just one of many stories and passages in the Bible that denigrate women and show the God of the Bible to be a petty, cruel psychopath."

"So what would you like to see happen from now on? Does God have a plan for elevating the status of women to equality with men?"

"No. As long as Christianity and Islam and other male-dominated religions continue to exist, women will be considered inferior to men. The only real hope is that the evolution of the human species will lead to growing up and getting out of the religion business. My Dad believes that women should rule the earth in all areas, but you guys are far from that reality. But if your species continues on for a few more centuries, maybe at some point you will evolve into true gender equality."

"Are you talking about the end of the world?"

"I'm talking about continued social and cognitive evolution. Nobody knows how this world is going to end. I don't know, God doesn't know,, and you guys certainly don't know. But it's in your hands. My guess is that the human species will ultimately bring about the end of life on earth. But I don't know for sure. Nobody does."

What he was saying went so against the grain of every religious teaching, especially Christianity and Islam, about the end of life on earth. Those religions were certain that the End Times were near, as they have been thought to be for centuries. Now I get it. The fate of the human species and all living things on earth was in our hands.

"That's it, Rog. The only hope I can see is if women take their rightful place and become the leaders in all areas of life: business, politics, economics, and in charge of the well-being of all people. Then, maybe, there's hope for the continuation of life on earth."

I didn't know how to respond, exactly, so I looked at Joshua and merely said, "I totally agree with you." Which I did. "Okay, Josh, just one more thing. Why is sex viewed so negatively in both evangelical and Catholic churches, at least sex outside of marriage?"

Joshua put his head down for a moment and then looked up and said, "Throughout history, Christianity has consistently regarded women as inferior to men. No matter how one tries to spin it, women have been seen, and still are seen, as subjugated to men. Paul of Tarsus wrote a mere fifteen years after my crucifixion that women were to keep silent in his churches and that men are more important in God's eyes than women. Paul argues that women are morally weaker than men and more likely to be corrupted and to corrupt others. The early church fathers were terrified by women. Part of that viewpoint had to do with Judaism, where women were basically thought of as temptresses and seducers of men. After all, as Judaism and Christianity both say, it was Eve who succumbed to the wiles of a talking snake and then persuaded poor Adam to eat the forbidden fruit."

Joshua stood up and began pacing slowly around the living room. He seemed to be searching for the right words, I guessed.

Still standing, he said, "Much of it had to do with sex. Since sex involved women, it was considered only necessary for procreation. That attitude was prevalent across Christianity in its early years and continues today although in a more subtle way. Sex outside of marriage is considered sinful and wrong. And considering the repression and subjugation of women, Christian Church history is one long arbitrary, narrow-minded, and masculine despotism over women. Think of the outcry when the ordination of women priests is raised, or the church's obsession with perpetual virginity and celibacy. It's sick, Rog, and it needs to go the way of the dinosaurs."

Hmmm . . . I wondered about the dinosaur reference, but I was at a point now that I believed whatever he said.

Chapter Sixty-One

Joshua took a cigarette from the pack on the table. After lighting it and taking in a huge drag, he said, "I need to make sure you're with me on what we're going to do soon. The Kingdom of God movement I began while here on earth before no longer exists. After I died, I counted on Peter, John, and my brother James to carry on with my teachings—passing them down from generation to generation. That didn't happen. That is perhaps the biggest reason why I'm here talking with you over two thousand years later."

I looked at him, puzzled.

"My disciples got it right and proclaimed this 'good news' about God's Kingdom for many years. They honored and treasured what I taught and how I lived, and they understood the implications of what I was trying to do. The Kingdom of God movement that I taught them about, though, was replaced quite quickly by a more popular movement. That's where Paul of Tarsus comes in. He was arrogant and prideful. He claimed that he met me in a vision on the road to the town of Damascus.

"But I never met the man."

"Never met . . . ?" I started to think, but Joshua broke in quickly.

"And that's the real problem. What people call Christianity today, in all but a few instances is not based on what I taught or how I lived. Within fifteen years of my death, Paul hijacked the Kingdom of God message and created a whole new religion—*in my name*! He was one of the first, and most successful, of the false teachers I kept warning my disciples about. He had his own agenda, and it had nothing to do with me."

I was stunned. He was basically saying that Christianity through the ages was nothing but a complete misrepresentation of what Joshua taught and how he encouraged people to live.

"Within two decades the original twelve apostles, the ones I personally handpicked to carry on the message of hope that the Kingdom of God was here—right here, right now—began to fade away, and a new Christ figure took my place. All because of one individual."

Looking right at each other, we both said his name out loud in unison, "Paul."

Chapter Sixty-Two

Joshua had more to say before we were ready to actually confront the guy in person; which was his plan, I was sure.

He looked at me and said, "Paul's religion was not what I taught. His religion differed considerably in origin, beliefs, and practices from my Kingdom of God message. His movement wasn't based on what I taught but on his alleged *meeting* me in a spontaneous vision, followed by a series of other 'visitations' over the next decade. Looking back at the letters he wrote, which make up over two-thirds of the New Testament, he never refers to me or my life, my teachings, or my healings—only to this mythical Christ figure he saw in a vision. That's what makes me and my Dad so bummed out and what has led to this artificial and distorted phenomenon called Christianity. It's a myth."

Man, Joshua was angry. "Rightfully so," I thought. I mean, his followers spent over three years with him, listened to him teach, watched him perform signs and wonders, ate with him every day, and then watched as he was horribly crucified. Paul's message had nothing to do with Joshua the Jewish rabbi teaching about the Kingdom of God. For Paul it was just "Believe that Jesus is God, and you will have eternal life." *What?* No wonder Joshua was angry.

The way I saw it, Paul's religion was certainly more attractive than Joshua's Jewish-based requirements to establish the Kingdom of God on earth. It fit right in with all the other exciting and entertaining Roman mystery religions and deities of the day. I remember reading years ago that, within a decade of Paul's "Vision of Christ," he had attracted thousands of followers, many of them quite wealthy, and was put by many on a pedestal as equal to . . . to whom? God?

The irony of it was stunning.

Joshua broke into my thoughts, "Long after Paul's death in AD 64, the movement he began had all the bells and whistles required of any successful venture. His movement continued to grow exponentially over the next three centuries, culminating with the Roman emperor Constantine's declaration that Paul's version of Christianity was *the* official religion of the Roman Empire. Paul's brand of Christianity had the product: welcoming and easy to follow. What could possibly go wrong?"

Chapter Sixty-Three

I needed to think. Joshua was talking about going back one more time, this time to around AD 55, twenty plus years after his death and resurrection. He had invited me to join him, and I was feeling a bit uneasy. Joshua told Joseph that it was only him and me who would be going. Joseph lowered his head when Joshua told him that, but he accepted his decision.

What was I supposed to be doing while they were "chatting" together? Was I supposed to jump in with questions?

Joshua broke into my thoughts. "No, Rog, you're there to listen. I need you to tell the readers of this interview all about this guy. People need to know."

"What a recipe for disaster!" I thought. Joshua had just pretty much called the so-called apostle Paul a liar and a deceiver.

And now we were going back to see Paul in action! I was excited despite my misgivings. I was still puzzled by what Joshua had said. What was it? Oh yeah, he wanted to have a "chat" with Paul. In my experience, the word "chat" always seemed to have a negative ring to it.

Joshua and I settled back in at the kitchen table. I was shuffling through notes and questions, ready to try and continue on with the interview. He had a strange look on his face. I couldn't read him.

I had all sorts of questions bursting into my mind, but now was the time to listen. The three of us were still sitting at the kitchen table. Joshua looked at each of us and then said, "Twenty years had passed since the time of my death and resurrection.

Now my followers were getting older; some had already died. As the years rolled by, these stories that were circulating about me started to be written down about what I had said and soon became pamphlets, letters, and then short books. The Kingdom of God movement I had begun was starting to recede as Paul's writings began to get wide circulation. My simple message of loving God, loving others as you love yourself and taking care of the poor and down-and-out types, and what I promised about living life to the fullest—it started to become a mishmash of teachings, some true, some made up. My Dad and I were getting pretty upset at how deceptive and dishonest some of the second-generation followers were in distorting the most significant message in human history. Should I go back and set everyone straight? We didn't know. But my Dad is pretty smart. And we were curious. He said, 'Let's let this thing go for a while and see what happens.'"

I was staring up at the ceiling, fascinated with what Joshua was telling me.

He continued, "I'm not exactly sure if he was happy with that decision back then. But what has happened since then has been nothing short of disastrous: the formation of different Messianic cults, early forms of what came to be known as Christianity, and now we all know the history of the Christian Church on earth right up to the twenty-first century. Not a pretty picture." He glanced over at me and said, "But there have always been people, billions of people, actually, over the centuries who have tried to live lives 'right with God.' That's why he let it continue."

Joshua was headed somewhere with all this, I figured, but I was still in the dark.

Without missing a beat, he continued, "One person, in this case one single man, can change the course of history: Alexander the Great, Constantine, Napoleon, Hitler—the list goes on and on. But that one man in the first century, Paul of Tarsus, changed the greatest message ever given to humankind. Before I can finish this interview and tell you everything that I want to communicate to the twenty-first-century world, I need to go back and have a chat with Paul. And you're coming with me so that you can see for yourself the virtually unimaginable *damage* that the man has done to God's Dream. Plus I might need a witness."

Joshua got up from the kitchen table and walked the short distance into the living room. I followed suit. Joseph stayed at the table.

Joshua faced me and said, "Are you ready for this, Rog? Take my hands."

As soon as I took his hands, the whirlwind started immediately. I lost consciousness. The last thought I remember having was, "Paul!"

Chapter Sixty-Four

We had a relatively soft landing (no broken bones or lacerations, anyway) in the middle of a field. I had yet to figure out who or what determined where we would land on these transportations into the past (or back to the future), so I guess I was just happy not to be banged up.

I looked around for Joshua and saw him sitting up about ten yards away, holding his head in his hands as if he had landed on a rock or something. It was daylight, and my eyes quickly focused. As I was looking over at Joshua, I noticed he had a big goofy grin on his face.

"Hmmm," I wondered. "Is it disrespectful to call him goofy looking?" I brushed the thought from my mind and scrambled over to where he was sitting up. He was laughing now, and I noticed he was holding something in his right hand.

"Really?" I thought. "Had he really landed face down in donkey shit?" He had! I couldn't help it; I burst into laughter! He looked at me with shit on his hands and traces of it on his forehead and just doubled over in laughter. He was laughing so hard that he started choking.

"Oh, great!" I thought. "Now I was going to be the one who has to save the life of the Son of God?" I didn't relish the thought of having to give him mouth-to-mouth . . .

"Hey! Little help over here?" he managed to croak out in between great gulps of air and laughter.

I quickly fished around for my cell phone to take a—wait a minute! I had my robe on again. No cell phone available.

"It probably wouldn't get reception out here anyway," I thought stupidly.

I started to search for something, anything, in the pockets of my robe. What? What was *this*? It turned out that I did have a—what? A roll of toilet paper? "What the . . ." Ditching my thoughts, I pulled it out and gave it to Joshua, who wasn't smelling all that great.

"Thanks, Rog," he said. "Now can you dig through my robe and see if you can find my flask of wine?"

I did. He rolled off a huge amount of toilet paper, wet it with wine from the flask, and started wiping away at his forehead and hands.

"Quite the start to our latest adventure," I thought.

I asked Joshua the obvious, "Where are we, and where do we go from here?"

Without missing a beat, he said to me, "We're not far from the city of Antioch, and it's about twenty years after my death and resurrection. Somewhere around AD 55, if I figured it right." He looked around the countryside and said, "If I'm right, and I usually am, Antioch should be right over that group of hills."

"Hmmm," I wondered. "Couldn't find the right bearings so that *we wouldn't have to walk so far*?" I thought quietly to myself.

Not quietly enough, it turned out.

"C'mon, Rog, you could use a little exercise."

So we set off for Antioch where, I suspected, a man named Paul of Tarsus was holed up.

Chapter Sixty-Five

It was going to be a good two-hour walk from where we landed, so I figured I'd try to find out what Joshua had in mind when he said he wanted to have a "chat" with Paul. It didn't sound like it was going to be a *friendly* chat either. From his demeanor and what he had already told me, I was pretty sure that he was going to give this Paul guy a piece of his mind.

As we walked along the rocky trail with a few stragglers, I decided to pursue it. I asked him, "So what's the deal with this Paul, anyway?"

He kept walking for a moment and then stopped and said to me, "You know a bit about Paul, Rog. Remember your Bible-college days? What do you remember?"

I thought about that for a minute. "Well, I do remember that Paul of Tarsus is credited with writing at least two-thirds of the New Testament," I answered proudly. "And that the letter he wrote to your followers in the city of Galatia was the first letter he wrote."

Hmmm, I even surprised myself with what I was remembering.

"I also remember that he never hung out with you while you were here. He didn't know your twelve apostles and didn't actually meet them until around three years after he had his famous epiphany where you appeared to him on the road to Damascus. At least that part's right, right?"

Joshua smiled at me and said, "No, that's not right. Like I told you earlier, I never met the man."

His smile turned to stone.

"This will be the first time. Tell me more about what you know about him."

I was dumbfounded. "Why did Joshua keep asking me to tell him about Paul?" I wondered. "Well, his letters form the basis for what most Christians believe about *you*, right?"

"Right, but it's not all right," he responded. "That's why I want to talk to him. Something went terribly wrong as soon as this Paul guy had his so-called vision of me on the road to Damascus. He hijacked the movement that I started, which was to teach people how to bring the Kingdom of God to *earth* as it is in heaven."

Well, I'd heard that before—that teaching about his Dad's Kingdom—but I was astonished to hear him dissing Paul. Something *was* terribly wrong, but I wasn't sure why.

Joshua continued, "Recall that he never hung out with us, never heard me teach, never saw me heal people, wasn't there for my crucifixion, and never saw me after my Dad raised me from the dead. I didn't know the man."

"So you never appeared to him in a vision on the road to Damascus?" I asked in wonder.

"No. I don't know *what* happened to him or what he allegedly saw. I have my suspicions, though," he said.

We started walking again, and he asked me to keep talking about what I remembered about Paul from Bible college.

"Well," I continued tentatively. "I remember that he was a prolific letter writer. I remember thinking that he was vicious and self-aggrandizing. My one-word description of him at the time was *vitriolic*. I could never say it out loud in my Bible-college classes or with my professors, but I thought he was a complete jerk."

Still walking, Joshua glanced over at me with that wry smile of his and one eyebrow raised. "I'm glad to know we're on the same page with this," he said. "It might get ugly."

"Ugly?" I thought. I figured as long as I had the Son of God by my side that I could do anything. Even confront Paul of Tarsus.

We walked on in silence the rest of the way.

Chapter Sixty-Six

We entered through the city gates of Antioch along with a small crowd of travelers, farmers, and shepherds. I was again reminded of scenes from movies situated in the Middle East with all the hustle and bustle of the marketplace. I was still trying to get used to the different sights and smells of the place, but at least I could understand what people were saying. After threading through the marketplace for a while, Joshua went up to one of the street vendors and asked where the Jewish temple was located.

"Ah, yes!" one man answered excitedly when Joshua asked him if he knew Paul of Tarsus. "He lives not far from here, but he's not home. All you see here are on their way to listen to him speak in the temple."

"Perfect timing," I thought. "Now I'll get to see what Joshua has to say to—"

"Hold on, Rog. We're just going to listen. Then maybe Paul and I will have our little chat," he said.

We weaved our way through the growing throng of people on their way to the temple. I could hear people talking among themselves excitedly. "What secret will he share with us this time?" I heard one man say.

Another responded to him, saying, "Yes, the man *did* meet the living Christ personally."

I could see the great spire of the temple dead ahead. We hustled in with the rest of the crowd, although tons of people had to listen from the temple courtyard. It was that crowded.

Fortunately, Paul of Tarsus had a booming voice. No sooner were we able to sit down near the outer wall of the main auditorium than a voice rose above the hushed murmur of the crowd.

"I am Paul, a servant of Jesus Christ!" he began impressively. "For those of you here for the first time, I have been preaching the message that Jesus Christ gave to me personally many years ago in a vision: that God has turned his back on the Jewish people and handed his message to all peoples of the world. I am his ambassador!"

"Hmmm?" I wondered. "Really? God has turned his back on his chosen people? That was news to me," I thought.

Evidently, Joshua was thinking the same thing because he sneaked a glance my way with a look as if to say, "Yeah, right."

Paul continued, "Twelve years ago I visited the so-called leaders of the Jewish sect known as The Way, and Christ told me then and there that they were wrong. I even spoke with James, the brother of the Christ, as well as Peter, John, and Barnabas. Not that I consider important those who are called apostles of the Christ, but we remained cordial. They have their brand of Judaism, but God has shown me the true message through sending me his Son to me in a vision. They were stuck in their Judaism, but I had broken free of mine, thanks be to God!"

His voiced continued to swell to a higher pitch as he continued.

"Later, when Peter came right here to the city of Antioch, I confronted him with his lies. He maintained that one who serves the Christ must also obey the Jewish Torah, even demanding that new male converts subject themselves to being circumcised! I told him firmly that, if that was what he was teaching, I hope that his hand holding the sharpened knife would slip when he was performing circumcisions, *so that he would castrate his own converts to his perverted religion."*

Joshua was getting visibly upset.

Paul continued, "I was born a Jew, but Christ told me in my vision that being a Jew could not save me. That is why Jesus Christ came to me and told me that the Jewish laws were no longer necessary to follow; only believe that Jesus is the Son of God, and you will be saved!"

A loud roar of approval went up from the crowd, both inside the temple auditorium and outside in the courtyard. "*That* was a message people could sink their teeth into: no pain and still gain!" I thought.

Joshua elbowed me roughly in the ribs. He stood up awkwardly, pulling me to my feet with him, and he started to snake his way through the crowd and into the courtyard with me in tow.

"That's why we're here!" he scolded me in a hoarse whisper. "Did you hear the vitriol and hatred in his message? Does that sound like my Dad? Or me? What, live as you like as long as you 'believe' that I am God? This is more than just bullshit. This is plain *wrong*!" he stated emphatically.

I was pretty sure he'd heard enough. We made our way over to a small outdoor patio table and ordered some strong Turkish tea. When our tea arrived, Joshua secreted his wineskin from where he stashed it in his robe and added a shot of courage into each of our cups.

"We'll wait until he's finished and then follow him home at a distance," he said. "Then we'll have our little 'chat.'"

I could hardly wait.

"Maybe we should just take the advice of the Beatles on this one and 'Let It Be,'" I ventured, with the touch of a whine.

"No," Joshua said firmly. "I need to do this."

"But couldn't you accidentally change the course of human history?" I asked sincerely.

"I wish I could, Rog, but I can't. Even if I could, I wouldn't. My Dad and I are in agreement on this. It's just something I have to do. For myself."

So we sipped our stoked tea in silence, waiting for the still-audible voice of Paul to shut up so we could get on with our business.

Chapter Sixty-Seven

He finally did. We got up from our table and watched as the crowd thinned out. We were just about to do the same when we got a glimpse of Paul leaving the main entrance of the temple, surrounded by well-wishers and a couple of hefty "followers" in front and in back of him, keeping the well-wishers at a respectable distance.

We followed Paul's entourage for about twenty minutes, followers dropping off one by one as they reached their own destinations, until it was just Paul and his bodyguards. They turned into an alley near the outskirts of the city and then ducked under overhanging laundry and finally entered the courtyard of an impressive-looking structure.

"Must be nice to have rich friends," I thought enviously.

We waited for a few minutes at the gateway to the courtyard. Joshua took a tentative step forward, looked back at me, and asked, "Are you coming?"

"No," I wanted to say. But instead I answered, "Let's do this."

So we did.

Chapter Sixty-Eight

I followed Joshua as he walked through the courtyard and through an archway into the house. It was big. I felt small.

The two "followers" we had been following blocked our way.

"I'm here to see Paul of Tarsus," Jesus told them firmly.

"He's resting. Who are you?" one of them asked.

"Tell him Jesus of Nazareth has come to pay him a visit," Josh answered.

"And his servant," I added sheepishly.

One of the followers motioned for us to follow him. He took us onto a small patio outside of the house. There was Paul, relaxing over a cup of wine and a cigar.

"Cigar?" I thought stupidly. It wasn't a cigar. It was a piece of papyrus that he was chewing on absentmindedly. He was sitting at a small table that contained all the accouterments for writing: a pile of unused papyrus, an inkwell, and an assortment of plumed ink pens.

"Can I help you?" he asked when we approached his table. He motioned for us to sit down. Joshua took a seat across from him, while I remained standing off to his side.

"Yes," Joshua started.

He paused for enough time for Paul to ask, "Who are you, and why have you come here?"

Joshua had a strange look on his face from my position. He stood near the table and stared intently at Paul.

"Do you know who I am?" he asked.

"No," Paul replied, "I don't recall the face."

"But you *claim* to have seen me," Joshua pressed.

Now he had Paul's attention. He asked Joshua suspiciously, "What the hell are you talking about?"

"I'm the one you claim to have met on the road to Damascus many years ago. You've built your entire following and reputation on that claim," Joshua responded.

Paul's eyes went wide with astonishment and then fear.

"No," he sputtered, "I don't believe you."

He knocked over his cup of wine as he stood up suddenly. His robe drenched in wine, he called loudly to one of his followers, "Get him out of here! Get *them* out of here!"

Instinctively, and without much thought at all, unfortunately, I grabbed one of Paul's long quill pens that had fallen to the floor. I held it out toward the burly bodyguard like Harry Potter would do with his wand. "Stupid, stupid, stupid!" I thought as the guard's eyes met mine. Somewhere from his person, he had produced a small dagger and was starting to raise it at *me*. When he realized that I was brandishing a quill pen, he stopped, turned toward Paul, and burst into uncontrollable laughter. Paul's bulging eyes narrowed as he realized it too, and *he* started laughing—at *me*! Seeing what was happening with the two of them doubled over in laughter, even Joshua's shoulders started to shake as he tried unsuccessfully to keep himself from laughing out loud. Unsuccessfully.

It was quite the scene. Here I was still holding a quill pen like a wand, and now all three were laughing spasmodically. Suddenly Paul's bodyguard reached out, snapped the pen in two, and held up the snapped-off end to Paul and Joshua.

An upheaval of laughter ensued. All three were now down on their knees on the ground—eyes watering, and volcanic laughter erupting from each.

And me? I stood there, still holding my end of the broken quill pen out at them. Only then did it hit me. Then *my* shoulders heaved, and my eyes filled with those good tears you got when you're laughing so hard that you really couldn't even control your bodily functions. Like when you're really, really *stoned*. My only thought was, "I should be videotaping this!"

After what seemed like half an hour, but which I'm sure was only two minutes or so (which is still a long time when you think about it), we all started to compose ourselves. Then one look at Paul's bodyguard holding up his end of the broken pen set us all off again. I've never laughed that uncontrollably before in my life. Ever.

Now what was supposed to happen? Could Joshua even speak? He could and did.

"That was hilarious!" he managed, almost losing it again. Amid the occasional ejaculatory laugh and sniffle, Joshua seemed to be regaining his composure.

Paul picked up where they had so unceremoniously left off.

"So who did you say you were?" he asked Joshua, stifling another laugh.

I was totally dumbfounded with Joshua's response.

"My name is Yeshua, and this is my servant Rahj," he said simply. Then he added, "But you know me as Jesus Christ."

Chapter Sixty-Nine

Paul stared at Joshua with his mouth open and his eyes wide. Then he turned his head and stared at me, open mouth unmoving.

"No," he said warily. "I *saw* you. You appeared to me in a grand vision with a bright light and a small earthquake. I *saw* you!"

Joshua slowly raised his hand toward Paul's shoulder. Paul's bodyguard, still holding his end of the broken quill pen, took a quick step forward, but Paul raised his arm to his waist, palm down. The bodyguard stopped in his tracks and took a step back.

Joshua put his hand on Paul's shoulder. Paul was considerably smaller than Joshua—bald pate, scraggly beard, and narrow eyes, eyes that now looked up slightly at Joshua. Paul's arms were crossed over his spindly chest, and it was easy to tell he was nervous and wary about what was happening.

Paul looked at me, then back at Joshua, whose hand was still on his shoulder, and said, "So this is your manservant? What—Rahj?"

"Yes," Joshua lied. "I asked him to come with me for moral support."

"Moral support? What's going on here, exactly?"

Joshua moved away from Paul and began picking up an overturned chair and then another while we watched. After the second chair was back in place, Paul's bodyguard lifted the table back into place and began picking up stray pieces of parchment, another quill pen, and an inkwell, lying on its side on the tiled floor with a dark substance oozing from the open lid.

After a minute of silence, while we straightened things up, we ended up all standing in a small circle. Joshua broke the silence.

"May we sit down?" he asked, looking at Paul.

Paul had gathered his composure from what I could tell, so he waved his hand graciously and said, "Yes, yes, sit—please sit."

Joshua sat in the chair nearest to him, while Paul took a chair across from Joshua at the small oval table.

"Yes, yes, you were saying . . . you caught me by surprise. I thought you introduced yourself as Jesus the Christ," Paul said as he let loose a breath of air.

"I did," Joshua said. "And I'm here to talk with you about the religion that you started over a decade ago with my name attached to it. I've never met you."

Paul pursed his lips as if using a stress-release technique. He was calm as he spoke.

"I'm not sure who you are, but you're not the one who appeared to me on the road to Damascus twelve years ago. So surely you must be—"

"Did you see the face of the man in your vision?" Joshua interrupted.

"Uh, no. But I heard his voice, and it didn't sound like yours."

"That's because it wasn't."

"Are you actually standing in front of me and claiming to be Jesus Christ? Have you been drinking? Or are you just a nut-case," he sputtered as he lowered his head.

Joshua cupped his head in his hands with his elbows resting on the table, staring intently at Paul. The tension was electric, and I could see a shadow pass over Paul's face while he reflected on what to say.

Paul brought his head up quickly and looked straight at Joshua, fire in his eyes.

"Look, man, it wasn't *you* who I saw—"

"I thought you said you only heard my voice," Joshua interjected.

Paul looked confused. "It wasn't *you* I heard talking and even—"

Paul seemed distressed. He took a quick glance at his bodyguard and then turned back to Joshua.

"Okay, look, whoever you are, I had an experience, a vision, twelve years ago. Everybody knows about it. The Risen Christ appeared . . . uh, I heard the *voice* of Jesus Christ, and there was a flash of light—"

"You already told me that," Jesus explained patiently. "What I want to know now is what the voice said to you."

"Uh, well, it said, 'I am Jesus. Why are you persecuting me?' That's it. Then, when the dust had settled, I realized I was blind! I couldn't see a thing. I groped around while my fellow travelers came over to me and helped me to my feet. Then I thought I heard the voice again. It said, 'Go to Damascus and find Ananias. There you will receive your sight back and become my messenger.'"

"What did the voice mean by calling you its 'messenger'?" Jesus asked quietly.

"Well, at first I wasn't sure, but by the time I found the house of Ananias and regained my sight, I knew that Jesus Christ wanted me to continue on with his message."

"And what, exactly, was his message?"

"He came to me many times in dreams and visions over the next three years. He was preparing me for something *big;* I just knew it. I decided not to go to Jerusalem to meet with Christ's apostles because . . . well, because . . ."

Joshua remained calm. "And what did he tell you this new message was?"

"He told me that the Jewish religion was obsolete and not to follow it any longer. Then he told me what I was supposed to do."

Joshua kept pace. "And what was that?"

"He told me to go to the temple and synagogues throughout the region and tell people it was no longer necessary to follow the Jewish laws and way of life. He told me to tell all people that they only had to do one thing to make sure to go to heaven after they died."

"Just one thing?" Joshua probed.

"Yes, just this: believe that Christ died on the cross for your sins and that God brought him back to life. That's it. Just *believe.*"

"So that's it?" Joshua asked. "Just believe that Jesus Christ died for your sins and that God raised him from the dead?"

"And you will be saved. As soon as I began to proclaim this message direct from the Risen Christ, all sorts of people, *throngs* of people, began to invite me into their homes, called their friends over, and asked me to tell them what he told me."

"So that was twelve years ago?" Jesus asked with pursed lips.

Paul was genuinely excited. Joshua was distinctly not.

"I learned from Christ himself in my dreams and visions that I would suffer persecution for preaching this message, and I have. I have started dozens of groups of followers in major cities. I write letters when there's any kind of discord or arguments in any of the groups I started, and I try my best to visit them in person. Of course, the original followers of Christ, the apostles, denounce me as a false teacher, but that only seems to add to the appeal of my religion. People all over the world now call us Christians. Pretty cool, don't you think? We even have our own name!"

Paul seemed to be taking a pause to revel in his accomplishments. Joshua looked at me sadly as if to say, "Hold on tight."

Chapter Seventy

Joshua was just about to take over the direction of the conversation, I could tell, but Paul jumped in before he could get started. He picked up a little bell on the table and gave it a quick shake. Immediately a servant came into the room, carrying a tray with pot of tea and three gold cups. The trays were laden with goodies: small cakes with ornate decorating, two bowls of assorted nuts, and a freshly baked loaf of bread stuffed with cheese, nuts, and pieces of fish and pork. Pork? This guy had obviously ditched the whole Jewish list of dietary laws. Pork was detested and deemed unclean by Jews. I made a mental note to ask Joshua about this.

I didn't have to. Joshua beat me to it.

"So let me get this straight. Your movement is spreading like wildfire, and you preach instant salvation by merely believing that Jesus Christ died for your sins and that he was raised from the dead. I can see why your movement is so popular."

"Yes, popular and easy to follow. We have a number of wealthy families who now believe my message and who contribute money so that I can travel and preach. I need comfortable surroundings because of the stress of traveling and preaching. It takes a lot out of me.

"Of course," he added quickly, "we also give a lot of money to poor people too. Can't forget *them*."

"So, according to your religion, if you believe in a certain way, you are certain to go to a place called 'heaven' after you die to live in paradise forever with God."

"Yes, yes! It's so very simple! That's the message given to me directly from the Risen Christ."

Joshua sat there, restraining himself as a dark cloud passed over his eyes. He said in a quiet voice, "Look, I'm not here to condemn you. What's done is done. I just want you to be honest with me. Nobody is going to know except those of us in this room, and no one is intent on casting doubt on your religion."

He was lying, of course.

"I'm just a man, sir; I don't claim to be anybody special. But I did have a vision of the Risen Christ twelve years ago. I come from a reputable family. My father was a high-ranking Pharisee, and he pushed me to follow in his footsteps. But I wanted to make a name for myself in my own right. My father was not pleased with my decision, but I gained the acceptance of the high priest when I offered to round up the members of this Jewish sect who claimed that their leader, Jesus of Nazareth, was still alive. And I did just that. I gathered a group of Jewish men, and we found out where these followers of Jesus lived. We burst into their homes under the authority of the high priest and arrested them. Most were thrown in jail, and some ended up dead. I gained the sympathy of the Jewish leaders, and I was regarded as a hero."

"Okay," Joshua interjected, "I've heard all that. But what I want to know is what you would like to see happen to your movement from now on?"

Paul went dark. He seemed to be reflecting on what to say next. A glazed look came over his eyes as he put both arms on the table and clasped his hands together. He quickly looked down and then glanced at his bodyguard. Finally, he raised his eyes to Joshua's and said, "The Risen Christ decided to appear to me to appoint me to preach his *real* message: that he died on the cross for the sins of all people and that all you have to do is believe that and you will be saved and live with God forever in paradise. And now that is *my* vision. I want every living person to hear about my message and to believe it. Only by believing my message is a person able to enter heaven."

"And if they don't believe or never hear of your religion? What happens to them?"

"The Risen Christ told me that everyone who refused to believe my message would be damned for eternity. He told me that God was preparing a special place for those who did not believe. The place is called 'hell,' and all who go there will be tortured with fire and will writhe in agony forever."

Joshua listened to him intently. After Paul finished speaking, he said, "So you're saying that the God of the universe is preparing a place of eternal torture for every human being who engages in thought crimes."

"Thought crimes? No, no, only for those who refuse to believe my message! Believe me, sir, there will be very, very few people who will refuse to join my movement. I mean, look at how many all around the region who have already joined it! I have thousands and thousands of followers already. Granted, most of them are women, children, and slaves, but I'm beginning to attract men too, some of whom are quite wealthy and who support my movement financially."

"And what do you envision will happen to your movement in the next few years?"

"Well, it likely won't last much longer because the Risen Christ told me directly that he would be coming back to earth to set up his Kingdom very soon. At that time all the wicked people, those who refuse my message, will be thrown into hell, never to be heard from again. Only the righteous will be admitted into paradise."

"When is this supposed to happen?"

"Very, very soon. At first I thought it would only be a matter of weeks or months, but now I know that he's delaying his coming so that my message can be heard by everyone. Then no person will have an excuse. All those who oppose me now will pay for their crimes in hell!"

"Doesn't God love every human being and want everyone to live in his Kingdom?"

"Yes, well, yes, I believe that, but it's not God's decision; it's up to every individual to decide whether or not to believe my message. When crowds hear my message, many join my movement because they don't want to go to hell to be tortured for eternity. To me, that's making a good decision! Who wants to spend eternity in hell?"

Joshua could contain himself no longer. He said, "I don't doubt that you had an experience of some sort on the road to Damascus twelve years ago. I still wonder who it was who spoke to you in your vision, but the real reason I'm here is to tell you about *my* vision. I had a vision too—a vision from God himself. He showed me the future and what is going to happen with your movement."

Paul looked uneasy again.

"What do you mean? Are you saying you have knowledge about what's going to happen with my movement? Do you know what's going to happen to me?"

"Yes to both questions. I, too, have inside knowledge. I know what's going to happen."

Paul had a wild look in his eyes. He seemed to have completely forgotten whom he was talking with.

"Yes! Yes! I am interested! You must be talking about when Christ will return again. I fervently believed that it would only be a short while after my conversion experience, but it's been over a decade now. Is he coming back soon? Next week? Next month?"

"No," Joshua replied. "He's not coming back. Ever. God told me in a vision that his disciples thought he would come back to establish his Kingdom soon after he was crucified, but he won't. Even Christ thought he was coming back within a few short weeks. But he, too, was wrong about that."

Paul's eyes were bulging now with anticipation.

"So tell me, please! What happens with my movement and with *me*?"

"Well, to answer your last question first, everyone dies, and you will too. But there's no need to fret about it; you still have some years ahead of you."

Paul beamed when he heard this bit of good news.

"As for your first question, your movement will continue to grow by leaps and bounds for many years, even after your death. In fact"—he glanced over at me and winked—"you will go down in history as the founder of Christianity."

Paul was almost apoplectic.

"Yes! Yes! I just *knew* that I was right! Christ told me what to preach, and I see it coming to pass right in front of my eyes! And now you're telling me that God has told you in a vision that I will be remembered for years! And, of course, that my movement will not die out."

Did Joshua have a method to his madness? Was he really just going to build Paul up and not castigate him for his false movement?

"And there's more. Your letters will be copied many, many times, and the world will know about them and read them. Your followers will elevate your letters to the status of Holy Scripture. They will be regarded as the 'Word of God,' equal to the Hebrew scriptures."

"But . . . but, I was just writing those letters to encourage my followers to stay true to my teachings and to deal with some, uh, situations that were arising in some of the churches I started. But you're saying that my letters will be regarded as Holy Scripture?"

"They will. And here's another secret: your religion will become the official religion of the Roman Empire."

Now Paul looked suspicious again.

"How can that be?" he asked. "My followers are being persecuted as we speak for being Christians. And my letters? They're just letters. I don't understand; no, I don't understand at all!"

"I'm telling you the truth. God told me in a vision everything that I'm telling you," he lied. "I thought you should know—that you would *want* to know."

"I do! I do! I'm just stunned to hear it! Your vision from God is going to give me the strength I need to continue on spreading my message and in my travels. I thank God that you came to visit me today and share your vision with me."

"No problem, dude. It is what it is."

Joshua pushed his chair back and stood up.

"We really have to get going. Do whatever the Risen Christ tells you to do in your dreams and visions."

I stood up too, as did Paul. He reached out his hand to Joshua.

"Thank you so much for bringing me this good news! May you be safe in your travels as you make your way home."

Joshua stared at Paul's outstretched hand. After a second, he shook hands with Paul. He had a strained look on his face.

"Good-bye," he said. "And . . . whatever."

He turned to leave, motioning to me with a nod of his head. "That's it?" I thought. "No argument, no words of condemnation? I really thought he was going to tear him a new one."

"Ready, Rahj?"

"No," I thought. But out loud I said, "Ready when you are."

And that was it. We left.

Chapter Seventy-One

When we finally made it back to my apartment, I went straight to the fridge to grab us each a beer.

Joshua picked his beer up off the kitchen table and took a long drink. He emptied about three-quarters of the bottle before putting it back down on the table. Me too—I took a long haul but only emptied about a quarter of the bottle, as did Joseph.

"I guess it's hard to stay up with the Son of God when he's thirsty," I thought. I heard him try to suppress a burp, and he did a pretty good job of being polite. It was so nice to know that the Son of God had manners.

"So we met Paul," he said with a sigh.

"Yeah, we met him all right," I said. "I didn't really know what I expected you to say to him, but it seems to me you kind of let him off the hook. I mean, he's the main reason that Christianity is in the sorry state that it is."

"Yeah, I thought about that. I was planning on calling him out as a liar and a deceiver, not to mention a narcissist. But it dawned on me quite clearly that you can't change history. You can try, and maybe someday someone will invent a time machine and—whatever. But for now it is what it is."

"Are you concerned that you actually meeting him in the past might have changed something—even something small?"

"I don't know," he answered simply. "Let's check out the religion section of the CNN website—just for fun."

I swear I detected apprehension in the way he tried to casually suggest checking out CNN. What if . . . ? I didn't know what to think.

I went to my computer and brought up the CNN website. The top headline was that Wolf Blitzer had interviewed President Donald Trump's press secretary about the possibility of using nuclear weapons to wipe North Korea off the map.

"You guys are in for some interesting times with that guy," he said.

I decided to check the religion section of the website. Joshua and Joseph leaned over my back at the computer screen. There was news about the pope's latest proclamation and a few other articles about whatever, but no significant change to Christianity that we could tell. I heard Joshua exude a breath behind me and figured it was good news that everything seemed normal.

I glanced up at both of them, and without saying a word, they took their respective places at the kitchen table.

Chapter Seventy-Two

I sensed that our time was running out, and a quick glance at the clock on the wall confirmed it. Still, I hoped we had time for him to talk about what he considered the current state of affairs of Christianity in the twenty-first century.

I glanced down at my notes and decided now was the time. I had thought about not asking about the falsehoods and atrocities committed by the church over the past two thousand years, but he did say he wanted to "set the record straight," so "Here goes," I thought to myself.

"Here goes what?" he asked absentmindedly. I guess he wasn't focused on my thoughts.

"I know you don't like talking about religion and that you didn't come to start a religion, but there is a Christian religion now, and you're here to set the record straight about all the bullshit that has been perpetrated in your name, right? So what's your take on the whole Christian religion thing now?" I was pretty sure what he was going to say about Christian history and the development of the Christian Church in all its diversity around the world, but I figured it needed to be said, so . . .

But I was wrong.

"My teachings and the way I lived stand on their own. I was an observant Jew when I was here back in the day, and I kept all the laws and dietary regulations, attended all the festivals, and lived my life according to Jewish laws. But my teachings go beyond the constraints of any religion. I learned so much during my travels before I began teaching in Palestine that I just figured what I taught was meant for all human beings, both the religious of whatever tradition and the nonreligious."

"So, are you still a Jew?" I asked.

He leaned back in his chair with a throaty laugh. After he caught his breath, he said, "No. Judaism is merely another religion—a man-made attempt to connect with God. But that was my tradition throughout my life; I lived and died a Jew. The thing is, what we now see in Christianity today, and which goes back to the end of the first century, is *not* what I envisioned when I started my teaching mission. If Christians throughout the centuries really wanted to model their lives after me, they would be faithful Jews following the Jewish laws and way of life. But except for Messianic Jews, that's never been the case throughout history."

"So when did the version of Christianity that we see today, and down through the centuries, begin to become a religion with your name attached to it?" I wasn't exactly sure what I was expecting to hear from him, so I guess I was fumbling around a bit.

"In the beginning, when I appeared to my disciples after my crucifixion, my brother James, along with Peter and a few others, carried on with my teachings and continued to be observant Jews. The movement I started wasn't called Christianity until decades after my death. It was merely seen as a Jewish sect. There were many, many other factions and sects within Judaism over the centuries, and my followers were deemed to be Jews who followed the teachings of their rabbi, Yeshua. That would be me," he said with a chuckle.

"So when did your movement come to an end, and the Christian religion begin?"

Joshua thought for a moment with his eyes closed before he responded, "When my brother James was executed by the Roman authorities in AD 45 for treason, well, his death marked the beginning of the end for the movement I started. By that time Paul of Tarsus, the so-called apostle Paul, had begun using my name as a cover for his own religion, which Christians have considered to be 'true Christianity' to this day. It's amazing that anything about my life and teachings survived, and they did so only because second-generation Jews who followed my teachings began to write down bits and pieces, mostly from oral tradition.

That's when Rabbinical Judaism was born because there was no longer a temple. Paul of Tarsus started his religion just a few years after my death and began writing letters to some small congregations of followers scattered throughout the region in the early AD 50s. But he had his own agenda, as we heard him say not long ago, and it had nothing to do with my life and teachings. In fact, he denigrated Jews and Judaism, which has led to almost two thousand years of anti-Semitism."

I was beginning to feel a sense of information overload. Much of what he was telling me was new to me (and I'm sure he knew it).

"Yes, I get that, Rog."

Geez! Oh, well, at least that cat was out of the bag, but I kind of felt like dummy.

"Don't, Rog. I know I'm telling you stuff that you might not be aware of, but you're doing just fine."

I settled back into my chair and let him go.

"It's like, most Christians today, and even through the centuries, know virtually nothing about their history, especially in the first three centuries. Well, actually, every century since then too, for that matter. When Paul's religion was declared the official religion of the Roman Empire in the early fourth century, everything had changed. Some of my teachings were preserved in various Gospels and other writings, but Paul really didn't give a shit about my teachings and way of life. Anyway, I don't want to get too deep into Christian Church history, but I do want people of all stripes to know that, at least in relation to the popes, cardinals, bishops, and priests, it's a very dark history and continues in various forms today."

That intrigued me. Even today? "Can you give me an example or two?" I wasn't actually sure what he meant by atrocities being committed in the twenty-first century.

"Yeah. But, like I say, it gets pretty dark."

"Well," I thought, "most Christians have at least heard of things like the Inquisition, the Crusades, murdering heretics, witch burnings, and that kind of stuff, so what is he—"

"But I'm talking about today. One example is that millions and millions of people around the world are dying from horrible diseases because of one teaching demanded by the Catholic Church."

"One thing?" I thought. Where was he going with this?

"Yes, one thing: their teaching on birth control."

"Okay, Josh, you got me on that one. What the heck are you talking about?"

"The Catholic Church's official teaching on birth control and the ban on the use of condoms has condemned millions of people to death over the past forty years because of the spread of AIDS and other diseases, mostly in Africa, South America, and many other countries where people really take Catholic Church teaching seriously. That teaching is, to me, obscene and inhumane. And that particular teaching is just the tip of the iceberg when it comes to church teachings, both Catholic and Protestant, on various issues while claiming to speak for *me*! That's why I'm here today, Rog. I'm here to put an end to these teachings and practices of Catholic and Protestant churches, along with the threats that accompany those teachings: excommunication, going to hell, ostracism, violence, and more."

I had to admit that he was making a compelling case with great passion. I had never thought about the negative impact of the "official" teachings of the Roman Catholic Church, in particular, in relation to such a seemingly (to me) benign practice of birth control, usually with serious penalties, both in this lifetime and in the next. But there it was.

Joshua continued, "The Catholic Church has become increasingly anachronistic over the past fifty years, and the pope continues to rule like a medieval potentate. And why? What we're seeing today in the twenty-first century is the beginning of the collapse of the authority of religious ideologies. With social media and the Internet in play, a growing social awareness of the history of atrocities, continuing into the present day, is causing the religious authorities to crumble. That's one of the reasons my Dad chose this time in history to send me back to set the record straight. Going back just to the end of the nineteenth century, Pope Pius IX declared himself to be infallible in all matters pertaining to church teachings and practices, eventually made official in the First Vatican Council. The real aim of that first council was kept secret by a small group of powerful men, including three cardinals, all of whom were members of the Inquisition. The end result? The pope was the *only* true representative of God on earth, and the reasoning went like this: whatever the pope told the faithful came directly from God himself. No questioning, no discussion, nothing—a maxim that continues to this day. When the pope speaks, it's really God speaking. And no one contradicts God!"

"Okay, Josh, I see where you're going with this." I didn't, really, but I knew he was trying to get something across that was of paramount importance to why he was doing this interview, so I figured I'd "get it" by the time he was done—which he wasn't yet.

"Do you?" he challenged me. "I only have time today to paint the history of the Christian Church with a broad brush, which was exclusively the Roman Catholic Church until the Protestant Reformation in the 1600s—with a broad brush. But I want to be clear on this. *What has happened in my name over the past two thousand years is a complete distortion and disconnect from what I taught and how I lived.* No church or religion has a corner on the truth. Not even close. And that's important to me and my Dad to get across to people around the world, beginning—it is hoped—with this interview and what results from it."

"Okay, bro, so, in a nutshell, *why* has your Kingdom of God message been distorted over the centuries?" I kind of thought I knew the answer to that question, but I wanted to hear him say it.

He did. "In a nutshell? Power and wealth. *Power and wealth!* Every human being since the beginning of evolving into self-conscious beings is pretty much *entirely self-absorbed*. My message was designed to break through that tendency to narcissism that is currently innate in every human being, and my message has not changed since I was here back in the day: consider others the same way you consider yourself, treat other people the way you want to be treated, show compassion for every person you interact with, be generous with your time and money, be the source for others, and most importantly, live a life trusting God for all your wants and needs."

"And did you live up to those standards when you were here two thousand years ago?" I asked naïvely.

"I tried, Rog; I really tried. But I was human too, and I had a daily battle with my own tendency to self-absorption, to be selfish.

And at times I was very selfish, and prejudiced, and distracted by the exigencies of everyday life. I was tired much of the time, both from traveling and teaching, and was regularly in physical pain. My feet were killing me most of the time. I longed to just focus on myself and my own needs. I longed to just be a regular guy trying to make it through this thing called 'life.' I wanted to fall in love and get married and have children and then grandchildren and to enjoy life as much as possible amid the mundaneness of this crazy world. But I couldn't. God picked me up by the scruff of my neck at my baptism and adopted me as his Son. I really had no choice but to try and communicate what he wanted people to know about life and how to live it with dignity. Even being adopted by God to be his Son had its pitfalls. In my little world, I was a rock star—an increasingly well-known and respected Jewish rabbi, with hundred and then thousands of followers in the Galilee region of the Mediterranean world. Sometimes it went to my head. It still does."

Man, this was heady stuff he was telling me. I quickly thought of my own responsibility in all this and felt this sinking feeling in my stomach that now *I* would have to struggle with fame and fortune as the one chosen to interview Jesus Christ in the twenty-first century. What he was telling me would be extremely controversial. Religious leaders and followers around the world would have their faith shaken (not stirred). What he was telling me to get out to the whole world was designed to change people's minds about religion, Christianity, the Gospels, his teachings and to turn on its head the whole Christian paradigm, challenging people of faith and no faith to understand the history of Christianity, and religion in general, from an entirely different perspective—from God's perspective. It was beginning to weigh me down as I thought about it. Underlying all this was the not-altogether-unpleasant thought that *I* might become a literary rock star! My self-absorption was kicking in even as I was doing this interview with Jesus Christ.

"Don't go there, dude. We're all in this thing together, and this is exactly what I meant when I said you needed to trust God to see you through this and keep you sane, if possible."

Stay sane through all this? That seemed entirely improbable.

"I want to get back to what I was talking about before we get off track. Here's the deal: within fifty years of my death, my Kingdom of God message was completely lost. After the Roman destruction of the Jewish temple in AD 70, my religion, Judaism, was forever changed. I grew up totally committed to my religion and mostly directed my message and teachings to Jews. But within fifty years, the way Jews worshiped, with the center of worship being the temple in Jerusalem, was transformed by the Jewish leaders—Pharisees, Sadducees, and Rabbis—who escaped the destruction of Jerusalem by Rome. Out of those ruins, Rabbinical Judaism was born, the same kind of Judaism we see today in the twenty-first century. Along with the destruction of the temple, what people believed about *me* began to change as well Not only were Jews considered to be my killers, but according to Paul of Tarsus, all Judaism was also to be repudiated. Paul, a Jew himself, began to trash the Jewish religion in the letters he wrote to small Christian communities begun by—yes, Paul himself. We know from Paul's letters that he had very little to say, nor did he care to know, about my Kingdom of God message. By the time he started his own religion with my name attached to it in order to gain more converts, thus more wealth and power, the damage was done. What became Christianity was a mishmash of dozens of smaller groups each with their own Gospels and teachings about me and God. Paul wanted nothing to do with Judaism, but he had a problem. I was Jewish through and through, my message was directed at the Jews, and many continued to remain Jews as followers of the Jewish rabbi Yeshua (that would be me)."

Joshua stopped briefly, making sure I was following where he was going with this. I was. I was already gaining an understanding of the confusion surrounding this Jewish rabbi named Yeshua and what happened after his death on a cross.

"Please, man, I need to hear everything in this part of the interview!" I was starting to panic but figured, hope against hope, that he had this situation in control.

He did.

"Here's what I want the readers of this interview to know: what the Christian religion today teaches, in all its forms, is wrong. Except for a scattered few throughout the world, no Christian understands my Kingdom of God message, whom it was intended for, and what it really means. No Christian today lives a life modeled after mine. I was Jewish. I was appointed by God to tell people how to live their lives fearlessly, joyfully, and to love unconditionally. And yet—"

"So what are you saying, exactly?" I ventured.

"Tear it down. Rebuild it. Or don't. Whatever. By the end of the first century, people believed that I had started a new religion. My story and teachings have been manipulated beyond recognition, which created a tradition with me in the spotlight, when the one I was shining the spotlight on during my time on earth was *God*. So not only did they make me a Christian, but they also made me God. Any group or individual who thought anything different about me was systematically murdered as 'heretics.' That practice continued through the Protestant Reformation in the seventeenth century, and we still see vestiges of it today. By the end of the fourth century, the price of theological unity, Paul's religion, was paid not just in gold and wealth but also in blood."

"Okay, Josh, what can Christians *do*?"

"*Wake up* and be willing to become conscious of the reality of God. People throughout the centuries have done atrocious and obscene things in my name; Christianity has caused division among people and nations, destructive wars in the name of religious fantasies, and an intolerance and prejudice that my Dad and I find appalling. The Christian churches around the world today, both Catholic and Protestant, have nothing to do with what I taught or how I lived. Either this interview will encourage Christians to wake up and see the truth about what has happened or it won't. But hey, ya gotta try, right?"

"Yeah," I agreed silently.

"You gotta try."

"Okay," I thought. "Maybe I could squeeze in one more . . ."

Chapter Seventy-Three

But I couldn't. Our time was almost up. I had kept my computer's recording device running through all the breaks and mealtimes, and this was no exception. We decided to end the interview over breakfast—almost like having communion together.

"First, though, Rog, *I* want to ask *you* something. You have three daughters whom I know you love deeply. But you have different emotional bonds with each of them. Right now you're estranged from your middle daughter, Alison. I can tell you this, though, Rog: she loves you very much! She just doesn't like you very much right now. But that will change."

My heart perked up when he said that. I so wanted to be part of her life again.

Chapter Seventy-Four

The clock was starting to click audibly in my ears, second by second. Still, I was getting more comfortable with the idea that we really were pretty much finished with the interview. Like, sure, lots would remain untouched, but we did a pretty damn good job of it, I thought.

"We really are out of time, Josh, but there's one more thing that I wanted to give you some time to expound on. I guess what I want to ask you to do is this: look straight at the imaginary camera that is filming this whole interview and tell your audience, whoever they may be, what is the one thing you want human beings to know before you leave?"

"Really, Rog? Okay, yeah, maybe that *is* a good idea, come to think of it."

I could see him smiling, and he quickly turned his chair a bit and pretended to face a camera.

"Okay," I said.

Chapter Seventy-Five

Joshua said, "Okay, here's what I want to say: *Life*. Nobody really knows why we're here. Many people don't know if there's a God or, if there is, what he's like, what he wants from us, and what we're supposed to be doing while here on earth. For most people, life is just a big mystery. We *believe* certain things, but we don't *know* much of anything with absolute certainty. If we did, there would be no need for *faith,* and it's *faith* that gives us *hope* for this life and even for after this life."

He paused, looked over at me, and winked. He had a "I got this one" look on his face.

"Hmmm . . . ," I wondered. This was serious stuff, so I figured the only thing to do was to hear where he was going with this.

"The one thing that human beings have always had is *hope*: hope for things to get better; hope that we have happy, meaningful lives with cool jobs, loving partners, and wonderful kids; hope that we stay forever young and in good health; and hope that we continue living in some way after we die.

"Yet most humans live with *fear.* Fear of death, fear of going to hell, and fear that you won't be liked by others if you reveal your true self with all your doubts, fears, and regrets. We didn't ask to be born, and we're stuck with our genetic codes, where we're born, when we're born, and what our upbringing will be like. There's nothing we can do about those things; they are beyond our control."

He lowered his head, eyes closed. After a moment, he slowly raised his face to the pretend camera.

"Me too. I didn't ask to be born, and I didn't choose my parents. My dad was much older than my mom, and I had four brothers and two sisters, all seeking our parents' attention and trying to find our own way in life. I grew up in a strict religious home and believed pretty much everything my parents and religious teachers told me. I played with my brothers and friends as a child, learned my dad's carpentry business as a youngster, and traveled with two of my brothers to various places for many years to learn new things and see the world for myself. After a few years of traveling around, I came back home, found myself in a bad situation, and got myself killed."

What the heck was he doing?

"I died young and never had the opportunity to get married or have children or the chance to grow old. But you know what? I made the best of it, just like you guys are making the best of *your* lives. Maybe you're thinking of killing yourself, or maybe your life's a bowl of cherries—or somewhere in between. You might wonder sometimes about the point of it all, but it's not hard to just not think about it. Maybe you've lived in poverty or on welfare your whole life, or maybe you grew up in a wealthy family and never had to worry about money. Maybe you went to college and got married and had kids, and life is okay for you. You'd like to have more money, but you're not uncomfortable—nice house, nice car, a job you're okay with, and a couple of kids who need a little dental work. If you're watching this or reading it, *you're alive*. You made it this far, for God's sake, so that's good, right?"

I couldn't even tell if he was joking around or being serious—or something in between.

"Maybe you're old now and just waiting to see what happens after you die. You're not scared, really, just ambivalent about it all. You don't want to hang around in pain for months or years waiting to die from Alzheimer's. You want to just get on with it. Billions have gone before you, so—whatever.

"Is that you? Like, you've had some good times in life, and bad times too; you've loved and been loved, and you made some really good friends and maybe a few enemies along the way. You have regrets about things you've done in the past, but there's nothing you can do about it now, so you try not to dwell on it. You're smart in your own way. You made it this far, so that must mean that you haven't yet got to the point of checking out, so you must be at least *kind of* happy, for the most part, when push comes to shove. Maybe it will get better; maybe it won't. Maybe you just hope that it won't get worse. You enjoy your job or whatever it is you do for a living; well, maybe not so much your job, but you enjoy hanging out with your coworkers, having a few beers, or going to lunch with your friends.

"Or maybe you're in a street gang, and you had to kill a member of a rival crew to 'prove yourself.' You're not happy about it, but you did it. Or maybe you're a fifteen-year-old girl who grew up in a foster home and got repeatedly raped by your foster dad, and now you're on the street selling yourself because your pimp boyfriend says he'll cut you if you don't. Anyway you're hooked on crack so you're numb or high when you're doing a stranger so you're kind of okay with it.

"Or maybe you found Jesus or Allah, and you go to church or the mosque and hang out with other like-minded believers and try not to think too much, and you even pray to that God of yours and hope, hope, hope . . . for . . . for what?"

I started to . . . I don't know . . . cut him off or something, but as I was just about to speak, he kept his eyes on the fake camera and raised his hand to my face. I got the hint.

"So what can you do? Much of everyday life is full of mundane things: eating, working, cleaning, talking with your friends, texting, watching TV, grocery shopping, playing video games, and on and on. But even as you go through the motions of everyday life, you can be *aware* of God in your life—that he loves you unconditionally and can turn your little world upside down.

"And that's what it's all about, isn't it? We all want to love and be loved, we all want to be cool and liked, we all want to live fulfilling lives that mean something. So we keep at it—enjoying life as much as possible, looking out for our families and friends, helping out when we can, hoping that there's more to life than merely dying and ceasing to exist." He looked as though he was done speaking, but then he looked back at the pretend camera and said, "And there is. So we do our best in this life; we do our best to love ourselves and others and maybe even God. We believe in love, but we're not really sure what it is. Here is what my Dad taught me about love.

"Love is patient. Love is kind. Love never gives up. Love truly cares for others. Love doesn't fly off the handle. Love takes pleasure in the truth. Love is genuinely happy when good things happen to others. Love puts up with anything. Love always looks for the best in others. Love never looks back but keeps going to the end. Real love always forgives. We only know a portion of God's reality here on earth, and what we may think we know about his love is always incomplete. But for now, until all is completed, we have three things to do: trust in God, live life to the fullest every day, and love extravagantly."

He reached over to my pack of cigarettes and lit one. He took a big drag and looked back at the pretend camera.

He stood up, eyes closed and his hands deep into the pockets of his jeans and said, "Fuck it. We're done."

Chapter Seventy-Six

It was 8:45 a.m. on Saturday. The past twenty-four hours had been so intense that I realized my muscles had been tensed up pretty much all the time since we first started. It was pretty hard to stay relaxed, I had discovered, while interviewing Jesus Christ.

But now here we were at the end of our time together. Now what?

Joshua stood up from his chair at the kitchen table and went to sit down on the living room couch. I swear to God, he looked spent—slumped over and breathing heavily. He had his head in his hands; he looked so alone sitting there by himself. My guess is that he was recovering his composure from his very last words of the interview. I slowly got up, walked over to the couch, and sat down. I just sat there for a minute, and then I was sure I heard him stifling back tears. His back was heaving gently, his whole face covered by his hands. He was crying. I slowly lifted my arm and put it across his shoulder. I hugged me hard, and he put his right hand on my shoulder, pulling me close. Now I could *feel* him crying.

"Josh, it's okay," I said to him.

I could feel my own tears rising in my eyes. My God! Here I was comforting the Son of God! I didn't have a clue what more to do or say. But being me, I said something anyway.

"Everything's going to be okay, Josh," I said. "I mean, think about the ground we've covered over the past twenty-four hours.

Sure, maybe we could have gone deeper on some topics, and maybe there are a few topics we didn't have time to cover, but overall I think we did a bang-up job."

Joshua stirred. He took his hands away from his face, eyes glistening. Still slumped over, he turned his head toward mine.

"Really, Rog? You really think we did a bang-up job?" he asked.

"I do, Josh. I think back on the things you said, and it was like lifting the veil and getting a glimpse of God, our Dad, and what this life is all about. You cleared up a lot of misunderstanding and confusion surrounding yourself and your Dad, the meaning of life, what God is like, who *you* are, what your Kingdom of God message really means, how we're supposed to live, and how to interact with others with respect and compassion. And so much more. I know *I'll* never be the same person as I was before we did the interview."

"Funny you say that, Rog, because I was just thinking the same thing. I feel like I've changed because of this interview. I do appreciate how open and interested you were about what I had to say and what I showed you in our travels. Like, I *knew* all that stuff we were talking about, but I never bounced my thoughts off a human being like this before. I think the closest I've ever come is when I was alone with Mary Magdalene, and those times were few and far between. So I guess what I'm saying, Rog, is *thank you.*"

"Do you miss her, Josh?" I asked.

"Desperately. I can hardly wait to see her again." He paused and then said with a twinkle in his eyes, "I look forward to watching you on the TV talk shows, Rog. You're gonna be great!"

"I do kind of look forward to what's going to happen after this interview and the memoir go viral, but I think I'll need some help getting through whatever happens," I said.

We both sat there in silence, looking down at the ground. After a minute or two, Joshua stood up and walked back to the kitchen table. I got up, too, and kind of shadowed him. I had no idea what to expect, other than my heart would be broken for a few days after he left. I really had fallen in love with the guy.

Just then Joseph came in and said timidly, "Are you ready, Lord? We really have to go."

I figured that was the last time I'd ever see Joseph again, and that made me feel sad. My feelings for Joseph brought me back to the psych ward where I had first met him. It had been a confusing time in my life, but after interviewing Jesus, it all became clear. God had sent Joseph to become my friend in the ward and to tell me what God was planning. He had guided me to this day, this time, and this *event*.

I suddenly came out of my reverie and noticed that Joshua had been somehow seeing my thoughts and images about Joseph.

Joshua turned to me as we were standing in the middle of the living room and said, "I'm not very good at this, Rog. This has been a unique situation, and now I have to go, and I don't really know how to say 'good-bye.'"

"Me neither, Josh. But I'd love to give you one last hug."

"Me too," he said.

With that we each took a hesitant step toward each other and embraced. Tightly. With tears.

Then I heard him say, "Dad, see Rog here? I want you to be with him in a special way while he finishes up his work. He means a lot to me, Father. I love him to death, and I can hardly imagine what it will be like now that the interview is over. Thank you so much for this opportunity, Father, to 'set the record straight,' especially doing it with Rog. It's been one of the coolest experiences in my life. Be with him in a special way, Dad. And I'll see you soon."

With that, he hugged me tight, and then, without looking back at me, he turned toward the front door, opened it, walked out, and closed it behind him.

He was gone.

I quickly went to the door, opened it, and said, "Wait, Josh, there was one more thing . . ."

But he was nowhere to be seen.

Chapter Seventy-Seven

I felt empty. He was gone. I went to my bedroom and lay down on the bed, pondering the last twenty-four hours and trying not to be depressed. I fell into a dreamless sleep.

When I woke up and glanced at the clock radio, I saw that it was nine forty-five. Did I just take a short nap? Then I scrunched my eyes and looked again. Oh, 9:45 *p.m.*! I had slept for a good twelve hours.

And I felt great! I sent out a quick prayer of thanks to, well, God, my *Dad*. I was exhilarated. I felt a new freedom and an intimacy with God that I had never experienced before. I missed Joshua like crazy, but I was at peace. It had actually happened. I had interviewed Jesus Christ, and I knew I would never be the same again. God was no more merely a vague concept, a shadowy figure that slipped in and out of my life. Now I knew that he was my Father too. I felt transformed. I knew intuitively that I would, from now on, live each day to the fullest.

Chapter Seventy-Eight

The next few days were a blur of frantic activity, transcribing the interview recordings, putting everything in the context of a memoir, and reflecting on everything Jesus had said to me. Sylvie was back from visiting her mom, looking delicious and treating me like a prince. I adored her.

Not her two cats, though. I tried to be kind to them, but most of my attention was spent on my dog Poppy. In my view, dogs were more, well, *human* than cats, or at least higher up on the intelligence quotient. Poppy was a smart dog most of time. She certainly had her "dog" moments too, though.

Four days after Joshua left, I was putting the finishing touches on this memoir. Now the hard work really began. Joshua hadn't told me how to get the memoir published, so I didn't have a clue how to go about marketing this thing; like, what reasonable publisher would believe that I had actually interviewed Jesus Christ? I began to feel anxious. This was my responsibility, I figured, and I needed to find out how to go about the task of actually getting it published.

I started to Google various websites. Many of them were for self-publishing: pay a lump of money to some obscure publisher, and they would do a minimalistic job of printing and promoting it. I knew in my heart that wasn't the way to go. I needed to find a publisher willing to take a risk, a well-established publishing house that would do it upright.

I began to catch on, from my Internet research, that I needed a literary agent. I found a website that listed literary agencies from all around the world. My plan was to start with US agencies, then Canadian, then British, then—wait a minute, how hard could it be to find an agent? And who wouldn't want to represent a book based on an interview with the Son of God? Then again, that actually could work against me. As it turned out, it did.

I finished my memoir in two weeks; I prepared a query letter and synopsis to send to literary agents. Some agencies asked for the first few pages or even chapters, and I dutifully started sending out inquiries. I was spending a lot of time during these early days talking with God, *my Dad,* and I was very optimistic that he would make sure that his Son's words would get published and somehow go viral on the Internet. I realized that I rarely just "thought" about stuff anymore. I was always thinking in a state of prayer—always talking and thinking in communion with God. I felt so free, so at peace, hanging out with God throughout the day. It was such a new experience and one that I hoped my friends and family would experience.

My three daughters were Christians, but I didn't know what that meant anymore. Were they experiencing the same excitement and sense of peace I felt in my newfound relationship with God? I could ask Daisy and Jordyn, my eldest and youngest, but there was still no communication with my middle daughter, Alison. My heart ached for her. I would do anything to be her "daddy" again.

Chapter Seventy-Nine

Within two weeks of sending out query letters, the rejection e-mails started piling up. "Something must be wrong," I thought, but I couldn't place my finger on it. I asked God repeatedly what to do; was I doing something wrong? Was there some kind of spiritual conspiracy to keep the interview from being published? I hadn't a clue. I couldn't get a clear answer from God, so I just kept sending out inquiries and receiving more and more rejections. Most of them were kind responses, saying that the memoir didn't "fit" with their agency. Didn't fit? How could they not—oh yeah, that pesky thought that I might be crazy. One agency did ask for the first three chapters, and I did receive a letter along with the rejection notice that explicitly questioned my mental state. It might have had something to do with my query letter that told the truth—that I really had interviewed the Son of God. I decided to excise that line from any future inquiries.

And then it happened.

Someone was knocking on a door that rarely gets knocked on—our apartment door. We really only have one regular visitor, Sylvie's best friend Heather, but she usually walked right in without knocking. Maybe a Jehovah's Witness? They always come in pairs, but only one knocks. I slowly got up and quietly looked through the peephole.

Omigod! *Omigod!* It was . . . it was my daughter Alison! I hadn't seen her in over a year. My middle daughter! The one who told me never to call her again. It was her! I was visibly shaking as I reached for the door handle. I opened the door to see her standing there—alone.

"Hi, Dad."

I was so stunned to see her that I couldn't even stammer out a greeting. After what seemed like an eternity, she smiled and said, "Can I come in?"

"Of course, of course, I just can't believe it's really *you*! I thought I might never see you again after what you said to me."

She walked into our apartment, and I motioned her toward the couch. She sat down, and I sat down next to her, but not too close. I sat there awkwardly for a moment. She broke the ice by saying, "That was the plan. You have no idea how angry and hurt I was when you tried to kill yourself. In fact, I still am. But something happened yesterday that I couldn't ignore. A stranger came to our door, a weird-looking guy with long hair and no teeth. He introduced himself as Joseph and said he was a close friend of yours."

"Joseph?" I croaked. My immediate thought—which I would never say in front of Alison, her being a born-again Christian and such—was, "What the . . .?"

I remembered that the Son of God had told me that he was going to send someone to help me after he left, but it was so vague that I didn't pay him much mind. But now—now that Alison was here—I started to connect the dots. Could it possibly be that he had meant Alison? I mean—well, it was all too confusing.

I said to her, "Really? He said his name was Joseph? Did he say anything else?"

"Yes. He said that he was an angel of the Lord. As soon as he said that, I knew something wasn't right. I believe in angels, but I've never met one. And this guy didn't look like anything I would have expected, and," she hesitated for a few seconds and said, "he looked like a homeless person from downtown. I told him to get away from my door and house. I was so scared! I had my two kids in the house, and I was afraid that something weird was going on with this guy. I started to slam the door shut, but it wouldn't budge. I was totally freaked out and started praying that God would protect me and the kids."

"Yeah, my grandchildren," I thought. I hadn't seen them either, for the past year and a half. It broke my heart not to be able to see them, but there was really nothing I could do if I wanted to respect my daughter's wishes. I knew she was hurt by my suicide attempt, but at some point, I just figured that she would forgive me and we could move on. But it never happened. Maybe now?

She continued, "He just stood there, smiling that stupid, toothless grin of his. I was praying that Curtis would magically show up. He didn't. So there I was being accosted by some goofy-looking homeless person. I was so scared."

"I can only imagine, my daughter. So what happened?"

I felt as if I was treading on thin ice. Here she was, in my apartment! I was both excited to see her and anxious about what was happening.

"Dad, I didn't know what to do. What happened next was something I've never experienced before. The guy on my doorstep just stood there, grinning. I didn't know if he had a weapon or whatever, and I didn't have my cell phone in hand to call nine-one-one. I was just so scared."

"But you're here now, my daughter, safe and sound. So what happened next?"

She weighed her words carefully.

"He told me something that no one else knew but me—*about* me, from years ago. I was stunned. Suddenly I felt calm, like a peace had taken over my mind. The angel's visage even changed. I came to the tentative conclusion that this might actually be a genuine messenger from God."

I instinctively moved closer to her, and she fell into my arms. We both burst into tears at the same moment. I could feel something melting. As we hugged and cried together, I knew something deep was happening. Deep. We had been estranged since I tried to take my own life, and I struggled with the thought that I might never see her again in this life.

But here she was.

After an awkward disentanglement from our hug, I took her two hands in mine, tears of happiness flowing down my cheeks.

"Alison. My daughter! My lovely daughter! I am beyond words." I said excitedly.

It was all so surreal! Alison was here! In my apartment. I thought, "What great timing. What *great* timing!"

After a moment of silence, Alison said, "Dad, I wouldn't be here if it wasn't for that angel. I'm still so hurt and confused by what you tried to do to yourself. But I knew almost immediately that I just had to come over and see you. Because of what the messenger told me."

As I was lost in my thoughts, Alison piped up, "The angel told me that I had to see you and plan staying with you for a few days. I made arrangement for the kids to be taken care of—your grandchildren." She smiled. My heart melted.

"Okay, my daughter. Can you let me in on the secret?" I ventured.

"Yes. The task that was given to me by the angel is to read through your memoir, help you with editing it one last time, and to be your muse. That's all he said."

My heart stopped aching. Alison was back in my life!

Chapter Eighty

With Alison's help I was able to refocus my efforts to get my memoir of the interview and our experiences published. She was also instrumental in going through the audio files of the interview itself, getting them ready, and when the time was right, posting the files on the Internet. We figured this was essential to get across the real message that Jesus Christ came back to tell the world. The audio files contained the actual voice of Jesus. Whether or not anyone would actually believe that I interviewed Jesus Christ was beyond us. But she got the files ready, and we would wait until my memoir of everything that happened was released—*if* it would ever be released! That was still up in the air as I continued my search for a literary agent.

And I did!

It came out of the blue for me: a simple query to an agency that then asked for the complete manuscript. I was beyond excited! Maybe, just maybe, *The Interview* would be published.

And it was.

Afterword

The book you just read is a story. I pretty much made it up, although when I first sat down to put this story into words, I must admit that I felt like I really was interviewing Jesus Christ at my dining room table. In a trance-like state, I wrote the first draft of The Interview in six weeks, staying up into the wee hours every night and just trying to (barely) attend to my personal hygiene. My girlfriend Sylvie helped me out in that department by not leaving me. During that six-week period, I would excitedly share with her what Jesus told me during our interview, including the time travel experiences back to first century Palestine. She was nonplussed with it all, but she put on her game face and went along with it. Thanks, babe.

I decided to write this story because I am convinced that most Christians, or followers of any religion for that matter, have very little idea why they believe what they believe. The Interview invites readers to reflect on that. I figured my story would be controversial, but that wasn't on my mind when I was writing it. I had learned early on in life to question everything and to follow the evidence wherever it lead me, whether it be scientific or theological or anything in-between. That maxim has served me well, I believe, and my story is a result of following it.

During the two decades I spent in the evangelical Christian bubble, I couldn't shake the feeling that something was drastically wrong with the basic beliefs of Christianity. One God but with three personalities? Jesus Christ was one of those personalities? The Bible was written by the Creator of the Universe? For those of you who take the Bible seriously, have you really read it? All of it? Is that really the best the God of the Universe could do? Maybe a simple addition to the Bible would suffice: "Thou shalt not enslave, murder, torture, disrespect, denigrate, traffic, buy, sell, injure, or otherwise harm any human being." There, that's better. Maybe throw in all living creatures for good measure.

I know a lot about the Bible. I earned a B.A. in Biblical Literature in the seventies at a conservative Bible college, and I learned how to read Greek and Hebrew. That turned out to be a blessing and a curse. One can experience great comfort living in a bubble; and certainty. My personal research over the next ten years after Bible college were revelatory. I started reading textual critics of the New Testament such as Bart Ehrman, Marcus Borg, and Elaine Pagels. I read the Gospel of Thomas and the Gospel According to Mary Magdalene. I relied heavily on my training in Greek and the research of the best Greek scholars to figure out what really came out of the mouth of Jesus of Nazareth and what was likely added to his teachings by the gospel writers Matthew, Mark, Luke, and John. Anyway, unless you turned right to the Afterword before reading my story, you already know what I believe.

Few historians of early Christianity doubt that Jesus of Nazareth is a historical figure, and even fewer believe that everything recorded in the gospels came from the mouth of Jesus. In The Interview, I relied on the Greek and Aramaic scholars who know a lot more than I do. My story is not meant to offend, but to make Christians, and, by extension, any religious person, to think. My story invites you to ask yourself: Why do I believe what I believe?

The answer to that question can have real-life consequences. Findings from the PEW Research Institute, authors Sam Harris, Richard Dawkins and the late Christopher Hitchens, and my own personal research over the years have convinced me that what one believes about God and the metaphysical strongly influences how one lives her or his life. That can be both a comforting and a terrifying thought.

Finally, if you read the book before reading this Afterword, you already know that I present Jesus of Nazareth as completely human. You also know why Saul of Tarsus (a.k.a. the Apostle

Paul), is not very high on my "friends" list. In fact, he's nowhere on that list. You're invited to make up your own mind about these matters, if you care, which some readers will and other readers won't. That doesn't matter to me. What does matter to me is that you enjoyed my story and feel that it was worth the money you paid for my debut novel. I hope you had a blast reading The Interview and that you recommend it to your friends.

Who knows? Perhaps God will decide to send Christ back for one more visit . . .

Acknowledgments

Where to begin? After writing two academic books, I set my sights on my debut novel. Writing fiction is a horse of a different color compared to academic writing, and many, many people helped make The Interview possible. But the question presses: Where do I even begin?

Perhaps with a few words of prelude. Few historians today doubt that there was an itinerant Jewish rabbi from the small town of Nazareth who traveled throughout Galilee (present-day Israel) around two thousand years ago, preaching about the Kingdom of God and a message of loving your neighbor and treating others the way you would like to be treated. He was one of many Messiah-claimants during a turbulent time in Jewish history while under the iron rule of the Roman Empire and trying to maintain their religion, identity, and hope for a better future. The Interview presents this historical figure as completely human; stripped of all the theological layers of legend and divinity.

Okay, where was I? Oh, yeah, the acknowledgments.

First, and foremost, I want to express my appreciation and thanks to Holly Lorincz, Founder and Director of Lorincz Editorial Services. When she was an agent with the MacGregor Literary Agency, she was my first cheerleader and head encourager.

Kate MacGregor, my editor on the first draft of the manuscript, deserves credit for helping me to understand what a story is. Her insights and suggestions were invaluable. Thanks so much, you guys! Kate's dad, Chip MacGregor of the MacGregor Literary Agency, also offered me much encouragement and inspiration on this journey of writing.

My amazing girlfriend, Sylvie Menard, put up with all my bullshit for three years while writing The Interview. Even when I believed that I really was interviewing Jesus Christ at our kitchen table for hours on end, she encouraged me. I do love her with all the madness in my soul! Her best friend, Heather Whidden, always had my back during some very difficult times during the writing process for which I will be forever grateful.

Other close friends listened to my rants about What Jesus just told me!: Derek Ormerod, whose sense of humor and endless positivity and vitality has enriched my life; Marek Krasuski for his friendship and for actually reading a really crappy first draft of my novel without ditching me; to Dr. Moira Ferguson for helping me maintain my sanity over the years (you almost succeeded, girl!), and to Dr. Brian Donohue (and his beautiful wife Wendy) for his insightful comments on an earlier draft of my novel. Brian's contribution can be summed up in one word: Giddiyup!

Thanks also go out to Dr. Lawrence Steven and Leslie Blais for their comments and suggestions on earlier drafts of my novel. I want to send a shout-out to Christopher Moore (author of Lamb: The Gospel According to Biff), for his encouragement and suggestions in a back-and-forth email conversation we had. As he wrote in the Afterword to his novel Lamb, "This story is not meant to challenge anyone's faith; however, if one's faith can be shaken by a humorous novel, one may have a bit more praying to do." The same can be said for The Interview.

Finally, this book is dedicated to my three beautiful daughters: Jennifer, Melissa, and Stephanie. The have brought me endless joy and happiness over the years, not to mention five pretty cool grandkids! I love you guys!

About the Author

Roger Spielmann is a professor of linguistics at Laurentian University in Sudbury, Ontario, Canada. Author of two award-winning non-fiction books (*You're So Fat!* and *Anishnaabe World*), Dr. Spielmann has a B.A. in Biblical Literature and studied Greek and Hebrew.

Once considered a darling of the evangelical Christian world, his journey took him away from organized religion, a change influenced by his study of the Bible in the original languages and his personal experience as a Christian. He became convinced that very few Christians really knew why they believed what they believed. His debut novel, *The Interview*, is designed to challenge what Christians believe about the Bible, the character of God, and the message proclaimed by Jesus of Nazareth two thousand years ago. This story is for doubters and wanderers, the spiritual but not religious, who want to know who Jesus Christ really was and what he taught. *The Interview* strips away the theological layers that have distorted the real message of Christ—the Kingdom of God.

The author grew up in Chicago and has three beautiful daughters: Jennifer, Melissa, and Stephanie, along with five pretty cool grandkids.

www.ingramcontent.com/pod-product-compliance
Lightning Source LLC
Chambersburg PA
CBHW030904060726
47591CB00005B/1415